The eBay Book

Essential tips for
buying and selling on eBay.co.uk

David Belbin

HARRIMAN HOUSE LTD

43 Chapel Street
Petersfield
Hampshire
GU32 3DY
GREAT BRITAIN

Tel: +44 (0)1730 233870
Fax: +44 (0)1730 233880
Email: enquiries@harriman-house.com
Website: www.harriman-house.com

Second edition published in 2005
First published in Great Britain in 2004
Copyright Harriman House Ltd

ISBN 1-8975-9759-2

British Library Cataloguing in Publication Data
A CIP catalogue record for this book can be obtained from the British
Library.

Printed and bound by Biddles Ltd, King's Lynn

Contents

About the author

David Belbin is the author of more than thirty novels for Young Adults, including *Festival, The Last Virgin, Denial* and *The Beat* series. His work has been translated into twenty languages. He has also scripted stories about social issues for UNICEF's mass circulation Children's Rights comics.

David works part time as programme leader of Nottingham Trent University's MA in Creative Writing, one of the UK's longest established postgraduate writing courses.

An eBay user since 1999, David buys and sells in roughly equal proportions and has, at the time of writing, a 100% positive feedback record. Since the publication of the first edition of *The eBay Book*, he has appeared widely on radio and television, gaining a reputation as an eBay guru. An inveterate music collector, he spends much of his spare time going to gigs and movies. He also likes cycling, cooking, comics and Coronation Street.

This is his first non-fiction book.

Prologue

This book is divided into three parts:

1. Part One

Part One provides a general overview of eBay, describing how different people use the site and giving a little of its history. If you want to start using eBay at once, skip this section and go straight to Part Two.

2. Part Two

Part Two consists of ten sections telling you everything you need to know to get going on eBay as either a buyer or a seller. There are also three case studies that will be of most use when you've already had a go at buying and/or selling.

If you only want to sell, I'd still urge you to read the section on buying first, as you'll pick up plenty of tips about how eBay works and what buyers expect from sellers. If you only intend to buy for the time being, you can skip some of the sections on selling, but may still find useful information if you skim them.

3. Part Three

The last section consists of the book's appendices, which contain useful information on fees, surcharges, tax, and bid increments, as well as a glossary of the most common terms used on eBay and a refresher list of the top ten tips for buying and selling.

Advice on avoiding fraud is given throughout. There are plenty of screenshots to help you follow how eBay works. Note that eBay is constantly developing and the site can look different depending on which internet browser you use. This is a revised, expanded version of *The eBay Book*, incorporating changes made since the first edition in June 2004. That said, the basic principles of eBay remain the same, and most changes turn out to be improvements – indeed, many eBay pages now highlight tips given in this book. It should only take a moment or two to work out what you need to do in any situation.

I'm a regular eBay user, not an expert or addict. The only real criticism made of this book's first edition was that many of the tips I give can be picked up on eBay itself, or in its associated group forums. This is something I often point out myself, but that kind of research does require an awful lot of time online. *The eBay Book* is my take on eBay.co.uk, drawing on the way I use the site, offering case studies of other users and examples that can easily be extrapolated to cover different kinds of auctions from the ones I get involved in.

This book isn't aimed at full-time traders or eBay obsessives. It's for the general user who wants a readable guide written by someone who is completely independent of eBay. It represents six years of my own onscreen reading and trading experience. Many people have written to me, saying either that it's given them the confidence to use eBay for the first time or that it's greatly improved their experience of the site. I hope it does the same for you.

Introduction

1995 was the year that I, like many people, discovered the internet. A friend and I discussed ways to make money out of it. We agreed that online auctions were a really promising area. We even spent some time discussing how we might go about setting them up. It all got a bit complicated and I had books to write, so we never followed through. Pierre Omidyar had the idea and did something about it. eBay, the business he set up in his living room in September 1995, has, at the time of writing, over 147 million registered users worldwide. You can buy anything from cars to concert tickets, collectable dolls to computers, records to real estate.

In 2004, eBay.co.uk reached a tipping point. In the three months that the first edition of this book took me to write, over a million people registered to use the UK site. The UK took to eBay with a vengeance. Only the US and Germany have a higher percentage of members in their population. A year later, the UK site has just passed the ten million registered users mark.

New members want to be reassured, to be given an idea of what's out there and told how to avoid pitfalls. That's what this book will do. I'm not much of a manual reader. I tend to read the basic minimum then get bogged down by too much detail and stop. From then on, I just use the manual's index as and when I need to. I want to make the book you're holding readable from cover to cover, so I've

> "Most of the people I know don't use eBay. But all of the ones I've discussed it with are interested in doing so."

worked in some personal narrative and case studies from people I know. If you're only after the hard details, feel free to skip.

I started using eBay for a melancholy reason. In 1999, a friend died suddenly. Don's widow asked me to sell his record collection for her. It included a large number of rarities. I quickly found out what these might be worth, but knew I'd never get anything like their true value from a dealer. So I went to eBay.

I'd checked out eBay over the previous few months, but had been too timid to buy or sell anything. Now, however, I had a real reason to begin. To test the water, I auctioned a CD from my own collection: a rare boxed single that the Record Collector price guide said was worth £40. I gave it a high starting price of £20, the lowest price I would accept. A week later, it sold for £30. I posted it to France, throwing in free insurance, just in case anything went wrong. Two days later I received my first feedback: "Very very pleasant seller, beautiful item and carefully packed AA++".

More than half of the rare records sold, bringing in prices not too far off the guide price. They went all over the world. I found I had a new hobby, using my unmetered internet connection to endlessly browse eBay when I should have been working on my latest novel. I quickly got a yellow star alongside my eBay ID. This showed I had more than ten positive feedback comments. I sold occasionally, often accepting cash dollars to fund my purchases from the US (this was in the days before PayPal, eBay's widely-used money transfer system).

I've since discovered that my early experience was fairly typical. When I put up a bunch of eBay listings, I generally sell just over half of my items. They tend to go for about three quarters of what a specialist store would charge. Now and then, though, a couple of serious bidders go crazy and pay three or four times what an item normally goes for. Once or twice I've been one of those crazy bidders myself. It's probably not wise to bid on signed first editions when you've been drinking!

Over the last few years I've become a frequent, but never heavy, eBay user, buying and selling books, DVDs and comics as well as music items. In 2005 I got my turquoise star for 100 plus positive feedback comments. I've only attended one auction in my life, but I've followed thousands of virtual ones. I've been ripped off, made mistakes and learnt what kinds of auctions to avoid. I still have a 100% feedback record, the strongest test of an eBayer (as serious hobbyists call themselves). I still get a thrill those times at the end of an auction when last-minute bidders are suddenly outbid and try to get one more bid in before the curtain falls (automated sniping tools have taken some of the fun out of this, but not the unpredictability).

Until I got fed up and changed my email address, my inbox got several spam emails a day, offering me books or courses on 'how to make a fortune on eBay'. The book you're reading isn't one of those. It arose out of a holiday conversation with one of the publishers, an old friend who is a financial whiz but at the time knew very little about eBay. The idea of this book is to give readers the basics of buying and selling on eBay with plenty of tips, practical information and case histories. Equally importantly, it will tell you what to avoid and how to check out suspected cheats – both buyers and sellers, for the internet has given new life to many of the oldest frauds in the book.

This book will also give you the basics of how to run an eBay business, because once you start selling stuff on the net, you're in business, even if it's only in a very small way. Who knows, you might find dealing on eBay much more profitable than you expect. Or you could find it's a great way to track down rare items you didn't know anybody else was interested in. Soon you may find yourself selling spare stuff from the attic to grateful collectors who trust the way you've graded them because they've read your feedback. The possibilities are endless. You read a lot of negative stuff about trading on the net, but I have to say that the vast majority of eBayers I've 'met' have been great to deal with. This book aims to give you the confidence to become one of those eBayers, whatever it is you choose to buy or sell.

David Belbin

PART ONE

Guitar parts, pots, paving stones and trampolines

● ●

A brief guide to what people do on eBay

● ●

In 1995, Pierre Omidyar launched 'eBay's AuctionWeb', the site that later became known simply as eBay, by auctioning a broken laser pointer. AuctionWeb was an experiment in creating an open market that encouraged honest dealings. The idea was to make it easier for strangers to conduct business with each other over the net.

Six months later, Pierre developed the site's unique 'feedback' system. "Most people are honest," he announced on the site, "and they mean well. Some people go out of their way to make things right. I've heard great stories about the honesty of people here. But some people are dishonest. Or deceptive. This is true here, in the newsgroups, in the classifieds, and right next door. It's a fact of life. But here, those people can't hide. We'll drive them away. Protect others from them. This grand hope depends on your active participation. Become a registered user. Use our feedback forum."

The feedback forum was a big success, instilling the mutual trust that made users see eBay as a safe trading environment. The site kept growing at a huge rate. Listing fees were introduced, partly for profit, and partly to increase the quality of the items being auctioned. The company went public, making its founder and early employees fortunes. eBay saw off early competitors and potential takeovers. When internet stocks crashed in 2000, eBay was the big survivor. The company had a culture where employees treated the company's money as prudently as their own and there was an incredibly low ratio of running costs to profit. Omidyar had created something that worked uniquely well on the internet – "The Perfect Store", as Adam Cohen describes it in the title of his very readable history of eBay up to 2002. Since 1999, eBay has launched sites in another twenty-two countries.

I registered with eBay just after the UK version opened in late 1999. Today it has well over ten million registered users. Forty percent of UK internet users visit eBay.co.uk at least once a month. I didn't publicise that I was writing this book, just mentioned it to a handful of friends. Yet word got round, and I came across all of the eBayers discussed in this section (and more) by sheer serendipity. I haven't met anybody who's not curious about eBay. The users I've met are always happy to talk about it. They're not evangelical – that's not the English way – but neither were any embarrassed about the many hours they're spending on eBay: every week, or even every day.

Case studies

Rob

When they first discover eBay, many people get obsessed with the site, for a while at least. Rob, an old friend, has a few weeks at home before he starts a new management job. I ring him during the day while he's surfing eBay and we shoot the breeze about what he's been buying. At first, Rob only bought toys tracked down by his eldest son, but now he has more time on his hands and is exploring eBay's full potential for the buyer. Rob's hobby is vintage guitars. He bid on several, but kept getting outbid at the last minute. Then he figured out that he kept being beaten by 'snipers'. So he downloaded a trial version of a sniping programme himself.

> "Forty percent of UK internet users visit eBay at least once a month."

The first time out, his sniping programme didn't work. The second time, Rob succeeded in buying a vintage, beat-up Epiphone Coronet guitar for $150.

The seller wasn't prepared to ship outside the US – airmail costs would have been more than Rob paid for the guitar – so Rob got the seller to send it to a friend of his in Minnesota and persuaded the friend to ship it via the US Post Office, surface mail, for a cost of $50. Ever since, Rob has been trying to buy parts to restore his guitar to its original condition. Since these parts are small, most people don't have qualms about shipping them abroad. He's picked up a Gibson wraparound compensated bridge, a P90 pickup and a Maestro Vibrola unit from the US, all at great prices.

Kathy

Cartoonist Kathy bought a load of Midwinter crockery at a real-life auction and decided to sell what she didn't need online. It all sold (at the time of writing, there are 850 Midwinter auctions in the UK alone). She also managed to track down the three sixties plates she was missing from a Midwinter set, at very reasonable prices. She started buying odd things that took her fancy on eBay – a little wooden shoe, a medieval button, an odd array of metal detector finds that the seller obviously couldn't identify but maybe she could. Now and then she'll bid on some antique and the auction will go stratospheric. Somebody's spotted a real rarity. She's also started buying Midwinter and other kinds of pottery at charity shops and car boot sales and selling them on eBay. Now she's thinking about starting an eBay shop to sell off her vast collection of books.

Philip

Philip, one of the editors of this book, started using eBay for his son. At first he found it confusing: "I bid for some Football Sticker magazines for my son. I saw that the highest bid was £8.50 and romped in with a bid of £12. As soon as I did that, I got a message saying I'd been outbid at £13. 'Wow,' I thought. 'I'm going head-to-head in real-time with someone else.' So I went up to £14, and again got an instant message saying I'd been outbid at £14.50. How could I have been outbid, I wondered, when I'd placed a higher bid only two seconds before? It took me a while to realise how the bidding worked – that you bid the highest amount you're willing to go to, and that eBay takes the price up in increments. No bidder knows what the current highest bid is until he breaches it and takes that position himself. I completely failed to understand this fundamental point and it could have got me into trouble."

Philip soon got confident enough to sell on eBay. In his first auction, he sold a Precor running machine for £555.55, the buyer driving from South Wales to Farnham to collect it.

Clare

Clare discovered eBay early in 2003 when doing some research for an Art class she teaches. She typed a few words about 'Eames' furniture into a search engine and found herself led to an auction for an Eames-style hatstand. She won it for a bargain £25. The seller turned out to live only a mile from her sister in London and left it in the porch for Clare to collect. "The brilliant thing about eBay is it's so trusting"' she told me. A week before Christmas that year, desperate for an idea for a present for her husband, Roger, she typed the word 'theramin' into the eBay search box and found a seller in Australia advertising a 'make your own theramin' kit at the 'Buy It Now' price of sixty pounds. It arrived a week later. Clare averages half an hour a night on eBay. She and Roger mainly use eBay to buy vinyl records and books, rarely paying more than a fiver for an item. By seeking out stuff that isn't in high demand, they often get items for the starting bid.

This year, they've started selling on eBay, too: a harmonium and an exercise bike. "What I like about eBay is you either sell something or you don't," Clare says. "It's better than putting a small ad in the paper where you get a stream of phone calls and people coming round. On eBay, you only have to deal with one person, the buyer." She finds it fascinating for other reasons. "On auctions I'm interested in, I'll sometimes check out feedback and use the item numbers to see what bidders have bought. The information can be useful to me as a buyer, but I mainly do it because how buyers use eBay, even down to what user ID they choose, gives such a fascinating snapshot of people's lives."

Paul

Paul works as a building contractor. He's sold tons of stuff on eBay. Literally. The most unusual thing he sold was a bunch of paving slabs. Nothing special about them, just paving slabs. He was refurbishing some paving, so took up the old slabs and sold them for use as hard core or crazy paving, 'buyer collect' only. The buyer came from Norfolk and found that he couldn't fit them all in his transit van. So he took the first lot home. A fortnight later, he drove all the way back to Stevenage for the second lot – total cost, thirty quid. It would have cost Paul a hundred quid to take them away in a skip.

Another time, Paul auctioned a car bumper. This guy bid on it, drove over from South London to look at it, took a look at the bumper and said "I don't think I'll bother" and drove off. He retracted his bid the next day but the bumper sold anyhow.

The biggest deal Paul did was when he sold one of his stock cars. He put it on eBay with a reserve of £4,500. One buyer emailed offering him £4,000 for it. Paul refused, but when the car didn't reach the reserve, he sold it to the guy off eBay for the offered price, saving on fees. The strangest deal Paul did was for two mobile boilers he'd had hanging around for years. He'd meant to do them up but never got round to it, so put them on eBay for a

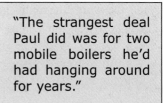

"The strangest deal Paul did was for two mobile boilers he'd had hanging around for years."

starting bid of £200 the pair, 'buyer collect'. A guy from the USA paid £440 and said he was going to ship them to Romania. He sent someone round with the cash. This guy said he'd be back when he'd sorted out the shipping. Several weeks later, the boilers were still there.

Paul's been using eBay for three months and he's already sold loads of different stuff for pretty good prices. The last thing he sold was an old Toyota car he never used. After I'd talked to him I had a look at Paul's completed auctions – most had hundreds of views. The site counter showed that the Toyota auction had been viewed an astounding 1501 times before being bought. That's ten times more than I've ever had as a seller.

There's a big market for car stuff on eBay. Winning bids tend to be lower than you'd pay a dealer but higher than a dealer would give you for your car in part exchange. Feedback helps to stop sellers concealing problems (although a large number of the auctions I've checked out are from sellers with zero feedback) and buyers are willing to travel long distances for the right car. The automotives section has its own, cheaper, listing fees structure – £6 for the listing, plus £15 in final value fees if the sale price is under £3,000 (see pages 163-167 for more information on fees).

Andrew and Paul

Paul put me onto Andrew and Paul, full-time eBay sellers with a large warehouse in Eye, Suffolk. Andrew was a courier, delivering leather office chairs, when he decided to try and sell one on eBay. He quickly found that on eBay he could get much the same price as a shop could, but without the overheads. Within a couple of weeks, his sales went from two or three a week to two or three a day and he quit his job, going into business on his own, working from his bedroom. Soon sales were seven or eight a day and he was looking for new things to sell. He found that high quality goods didn't sell as well as cheaper ones. People didn't trust the pictures as much, unless there was a big brand name attached.

Paul, a printer, started doing up pushchairs and flogging them on eBay. He and Andrew formed APS Discounts together. In their first week, they got their first piece of negative feedback. They'd described a chair "over-enthusiastically". When I ask for their advice to new sellers, they're unequivocal: "don't lie in your ad, not even white lies." The good feedback soon built up, though. Strong use of HTML in their ads made them look professional even before they moved from Andrew's bedroom to a warehouse. The pair also sell nursery equipment and furniture, trampolines and (above ground) swimming pools. They've just finished their first year of trading, during which they turned over more than £300,000.

Bid retractions are their biggest problem. People bid high, then change their minds. Or they blame the sniping software they use for typing in £3,000 when they meant to put £300. Getting refunds on the fees from eBay is a hassle and leaving negative feedback is dangerous. The bidder, even when they are clearly to blame, might leave a retaliatory negative. APS's positive feedback rating is well over 99% and they want to keep it that way. Most months, the pair pay eBay over £1,200 in fees and are now 'Power Sellers', with over 1,000 positive feedback comments. eBay gives some Power Sellers a phone number where they can sort out any problems with a real live person (smaller sellers have to use the slow, anonymous email system). The main problem APS report is fraudulent behaviour by rivals. A particular problem is bidder theft – people who email buyers who've bid on their auctions offering the same goods at a lower price. The crooks ask for money to be transferred straight into their bank accounts, then the goods never arrive.

A year ago was a good time to jump into the eBay pool, Andrew and Paul reckon, as the competition is getting tighter all the time. Large companies are moving in, catalogue shops and the like. These days, Andrew and Paul spend most of their time tracking down new stock. Plenty of manufacturers won't sell to people who trade on eBay, because they think eBay sales undercut the shops who are their main customers. But these manufacturers are dinosaurs. APS are careful to never tell suppliers that they sell on eBay, but their suppliers often find out soon enough. They tend to lose their scruples when they find out how much stock they're shifting.

APS Discounts try to avoid taking payment via PayPal, as the fees are too high. They prefer to take the buyer's debit or credit card details over the phone and charge directly. They never use reserves, as these put people off, and only occasionally use the 'Buy It Now' system. Mostly, they start items at 99p, because that keeps the listing fees low. They rely on the auction process to take the prices up to the appropriate level. It's very rare that they make a loss on an item.

APS pays tax and VAT. I've heard plenty of other stories about people making a living off eBay, typically flying to the US and importing goods brought back in a suitcase, but not declaring what they've brought in to customs or their profit to the Inland Revenue. They might get away with it, as both bodies are swamped with more cases than

> "They've just finished their first year of trading, during which they turned over more than £300,000."

they can handle, but it's still not too clever a trick. The thing about eBay is that all of your business records are available, online, to anybody who chooses to look at them. Many items expire after 90 days, but feedback lasts forever and tax bodies have the right to go back years. Nobody likes taxes, but businesses that do pay tax on their eBay earnings are understandably angry about competitors who don't.

Businesses like Andrew and Paul's may be the future of eBay, but are unlikely to cut out the small seller who is the heart of eBay. eBay remains a community, an extension of the spirit of the early days of the internet, with ideals that embrace an understanding, cooperative spirit. Profits aren't frowned on, but any kind of unethical behaviour is. There are even people who call themselves eBay vigilantes (see the Glastonbury tickets case study on pages 149-150).

> "Profits aren't frowned upon, but any kind of unethical behaviour is."

As APS has found, big business is bound to get involved in the world's biggest marketplace. At least, in an era where multinationals have more power than governments, eBay for the most part provides a level playing field. It also offers charity auctions and opportunities for third world countries to sell their goods to the first world without middlemen taking the majority of the profit. The site has sponsored projects that are starting to get third world sellers online.

Nick

Nick Talley ran a same-day delivery courier service in Stowmarket, Suffolk. He started using eBay in 2002, collecting memorabilia from his childhood. He got hooked on the eBay experience, rather than the objects themselves, and soon found himself spending more time and money on the auction site. Something had to give. eBay seemed to have plenty of buyers like himself and he had a storage unit that he was paying for but not using, so he decided to have a go at being a seller.

One of Nick's regular customers from the courier business was a poster producer. Nick saw there was potential with posters and gave them a go – bands and movies mainly. As that started to take off he set about organising the operation and formed a Limited Company. He expanded into photos and memorabilia and started to offer a framing and mounting service. Posters, however, remain his core business. After two years of trading, his positive feedback rating is 99.7% from over 10,000 individual customers the world over.

POP-culture.biz Limited keeps expanding. Business was doing so well that Nick made the tough decision to sell the courier service that he had started some sixteen years earlier to concentrate on the new business. On the Monday before I called, they had dispatched 113 items. They're running out of space to store everything as they increase the range of stock and Nick is considering a move to larger premises.

Another spin off from the poster business is Nick's idea to produce

Nick Talley, who won a charity auction that David ran for 'Children in Need' for Radio Two presenter Jeremy Vine's tie, here worn by Uma Thurman.

illuminated picture frames. Nick wanted to offer his customers illuminated frames to display the products that he sold but could not find anything available.

"I could see an opportunity so I set about designing and building many prototypes. A patent application was filed and the product was developed and perfected over the past twelve months. The result is the LumiFrame."

The LumiFrame is a contemporary picture frame featuring a self-contained "state of the art" light source that illuminates any image or flat object from the back and the sides. Nick will be selling the Lumiframes on eBay and at the company's internet store: www.pop-culture.biz

The long-term aim is to find a manufacturer to take on the LumiFrame to keep up with the expected demand.

Nick is a Titanium power seller, which gets him a phone support line and a 'power sellers only' community board that's occasionally useful. He protects his feedback rating rigorously. He leaves positives as soon as someone pays. Occasionally someone may leave a negative. In his experience it is usually a new user that does not understand the feedback system. He always contests negative feedback with SquareTrade (see page 144-145) to try and resolve any issues and get the negative removed. He has to pay a ten dollar fee, but it's worth it to maintain his high feedback rating and reputation.

Good organisation is the key to success on eBay, Nick argues. You need reliable stock and distribution. Not surprisingly, for someone who used to run a courier service, he feels that speedy delivery is of the essence. "People expect their orders to arrive promptly and we do our best to ensure this. Good customer service is key to longevity on eBay. If there is a problem, you should bend over backwards to solve it."

Rather than using eBay's listings tools, Nick lists with the 'Marketworks' (formerly 'Auctionworks') system to track inventory, raise orders and create listings. It was a steep learning curve at first, but worth it.

Nick's top 10 tips for sellers

- Remain customer-focused, reply to emails promptly and politely.
- Find reliable suppliers and build a relationship with them.
- Always look for new opportunities or angles.
- Change and test new listing strategies.
- Cost every part of the operation (right down to paperclips).
- Keep a close eye on cash flow.
- Set sales targets and monitor them weekly.
- Use the community boards for help, support and ideas.
- Take time out every week to check the competition on eBay.
- Stay the right side of eBay's many rules.

eBay – one of the world's largest economies

If capitalism has seen off communism, maybe eBay represents the best face of the victor. If you have a good idea and are willing to work hard at it, eBay provides equality of opportunity. It also has all of the problems associated with a new capitalist economy, with scam merchants trying to exploit every potential loophole and con any naive buyer foolish enough to drop their guard. For every scam that's closed down, two new ones spring up to take its place.

Buying on eBay can still disprove the old dictum that 'you get what you pay for' (unless you factor in the value of all the hours bargain hunters spend online). The main thing about eBay, for the small user like me who this book is aimed at, is that it's fun. Users don't count the hours. After a frenzied, first few months, most eBayers gradually reduce their eBay time to a calmer level. Until I started writing this book, after four and a half years as an eBay user, I averaged about ninety minutes a week on the site. I'd spend maybe another hour on an eBay newsgroup, keeping up with the latest changes and trends. Since finishing the first edition of the book, ironically, I've had far less time to spend on eBay and have done less selling, partly because I've been too busy talking about eBay in the media. I've published twenty-odd novels, but I did more media in the six months after *The eBay Book* came out than I had in the previous fifteen years.

As I write, I'm watching several auctions. Most of the collections that I searched for on eBay are long complete, but there's one particular thing I need, and the price keeps rising. Should I wait for it to fall again or buy before it becomes astronomical? Since the first edition of this book, I've become a regular user of automated sniping tools. I don't seem to win more auctions this way, but I've found that, on the auctions I do win, sniping in the last few seconds often means a lower final price. I'm not a gambler, but I enjoy the chase of an online auction. A few minutes online could save me hours in a shop. There are still things I won't buy on eBay. I'm writing this book on a new iMac, with a wireless connection. I bought the machine from my usual Apple supplier, who provides phone advice and sorted me out when I had trouble configuring my home network. I bought my photo iPod from them, too. But when I needed an iTrip, the device that lets you listen to your iPod through any device with a radio tuner, I went to eBay, and got one at a bargain price from Canada. For me and millions of other people, when we're after something pricey or unusual, eBay is the first place to look. The site, without a shadow of a doubt, is here to stay.

First things

. . . .

What is an online auction?

In a real-life auction, the auctioneer sets a starting bid and bidders raise the price until all but one of the bidders has dropped out. If the seller's reserve (minimum selling) price has been met, the last and therefore highest bidder is the winner. An online auction works to the same principle, but has two crucial differences.

1. Proxy bidding system

On eBay, buyers set their highest bid from the start, and eBay automatically places their bid at one increment above the current highest bid. This is called a 'proxy' bidding system. You can raise your maximum bid if you are outbid or fear that you might be. The big advantage of the proxy system is that you don't have to keep coming back to raise your bid every time someone else bids above it. The system will raise your bid for you, up to your maximum.

2. Fixed duration

The other crucial difference is that the auction ends at a fixed time. This time cannot be extended if people are still bidding. Often, as a result, a lot of activity takes place in the final few minutes of an auction. When it's over, it's over. As in a normal auction, the second highest bidder effectively sets the final auction price, rather than the winner. The auction ends automatically at the fixed time.

eBay's founding principle was to allow all buyers and sellers access to a fair price. Winning something on eBay doesn't make it a bargain, but there are plenty of bargains to be had, and I've picked up a fair few over the years. eBay appeals to people with a bargain hunter's mentality, but it's also a place where sellers thrive. eBay is a very cheap place to sell when you compare it to using other types of 'middleman', so both buyer and seller can do well out of a deal.

How an eBay auction works

When a seller puts an item up for sale on eBay, there are a few decisions to make. The most important are the title of the auction and the item description. The seller must also decide the length of the auction (the maximum is currently ten days), whether to set a reserve price and what the starting bid will be. They also specify how much they will charge for postage and packing, what payment methods they will accept, whether to offer insurance and which international areas they will accept bidders from.

> **Seller's decisions**
>
> • Title
> • Description
> • Auction length
> • Starting bid
> • P&P charges
> • Countries

The auction starts at once and the countdown begins. Note that the auction may take a while to show up in an eBay search. These searches are updated approximately every hour. As soon as an item appears, however, bidding may start. I've had bids within minutes of beginning an auction, although this is rare.

The first bid will always be at the starting bid, no matter how high the bidder's maximum bid. If there are no other bidders (and this has happened to me many times, as buyer and seller) then the starting bid will also be the final price. This is usually a good deal for the buyer. Things get more interesting, however, when another bidder gets involved.

If you decide to bid on an item, you have to go to the box on the bottom left of the item page which tells you the starting bid and the bid increment. The increment ranges from 5p for items bidding at up to £1, to £100 for items at over £3,000. For items between £5.01 and £15 the increment is 50p. Note that the increment is not set by the seller, but according to eBay's own rules (see page 169).

To see how this works, let's say there is an auction in which the seller has set a starting bid of £5 and that there are three people who bid on the item. On the next page is a graphic representation of the auction's progress, from the first bid to the winning bid. The oblong boxes in the middle of the chart show who has the current high bid at any one time. The grey shaded boxes depict the 50p jump from one bid to the next as eBay's increment system is applied.

Reserve auctions

One variation of the system described above is the reserve price auction. It works the same way, except that the seller has a hidden reserve price that the bidding must go above before they are required to sell the item. When a bidder's maximum bid is equal to or greater than the reserve price, the item's current price is raised to the reserve price amount. If the bid doesn't reach the reserve price, the auction continues as if it were any other auction, but with the words 'reserve not met' underneath the current price. With a reserve price auction, the listing fee is based on the reserve price, not the starting one. There is a fee for reserve price auctions (2% of the reserve, which must be £50 or over, see appendix on page 163). The additional fee is refunded if the item sells.

Payment and delivery

As soon as an auction is over, the winning bidder gets an email telling them that they have won the item. They will be given a variety of ways to pay, the most common of which is PayPal, which we'll discuss in section 8. Let's say they've bought from a UK seller and send a postal order for £12.50 plus postage. As soon as the postal order arrives, the seller posts the item to the bidder. Both are satisfied with the transaction and each leaves positive feedback for the other.

Legalities

Legally, a transaction on eBay is between the buyer and the seller. eBay hosts the auction but it is not a party to it and has no liability if either buyer or seller defaults. Clearly, it is in eBay's interests that things run smoothly, and it has put in place various safeguards, discussed in section 10. eBay makes its

Proxy bidding in action

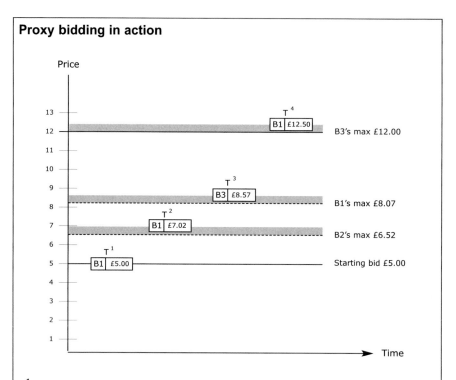

T^1 The first bidder comes in with a maximum bid of £8.07 (it's always worth bidding a few pennies above a round figure, for reasons we'll come to). The current high bid will be shown not as £8.07 but as £5 because the bidder has met the starting price.

T^2 Bidder 2 offers a maximum bid of £6.52 – higher than £5 but not as high as Bidder 1's maximum of £8.07. Bidder 1 automatically outbids the second bidder by 50p and the current high bid becomes £7.02 (£6.52 + 50p bid increment).

T^3 Then a third bidder comes along with a maximum bid of £12. The current high bid becomes £8.57 (Bidder 1's maximum of £8.07 + 50p bid increment).

T^4 Bidder 1 gets a 'You have been outbid' email. They can bid again, but must offer more than £12.50 if they are to become the high bidder. Let's say they offer £12.59. They become the high bidder at £12.50 (i.e. Bidder 3's £12.00 maximum + 50p bid increment). There are no more bids. Bidder 1 wins the auction at £12.50 – considerably higher than their original maximum bid.

profit (a lot of it, with over 100 million users, rising fast) from sellers, who pay a listing fee plus a fee based on the final value of the auction. Final value fees are just over five percent for items up to thirty pounds, reducing thereafter.

What's on eBay?

Before you decide whether to register with eBay, you may want to browse the site and see if there's anything you want. A mild warning: even if you only use the UK site, there are so many items in many categories that you could spend a long time doing this. If you have a dial-up connection, you may find browsing a frustrating way to use eBay. Don't worry, there are quicker ways.

Here's an example. If you click on the 'Consumer Electronics' category you will be taken to a page with numerous subheadings. In brackets, after the subheading, you'll find the number of items in each section. These range from (at the time of writing) 9,891 in mp3 players down to 443 in the now slightly outmoded VCR subcategory.

I'm mildly interested in getting a mini iPod mp3 player, so click on the mp3 section. I work my way through fifty listings and, when I get to the bottom of the page, discover that there are thirty-two more pages to go.

I can search through all of these pages, or I can return to the top of the page and use the search box that is an integral part of eBay – its own search engine, like Google. This box allows me to search within the mp3 players and reduces my search from thirty-three pages to nine. I quickly get a sense of what the going rate for a mini iPod is (at the time of writing, the new ones with longer battery life are in short supply) – only a few pounds less than my local Apple store charges. Not promising.

Searching and watching

As I'm a registered eBay user, I add a mini iPod that's currently at a reasonable price to my eBay 'watching page'. Whenever I go to this page now, I'll be able to see the price on this and any other auction I'm keeping an eye on. You can't have a full watching page until you're registered, but can watch up to ten items as a guest.

Fig 1. eBay categories

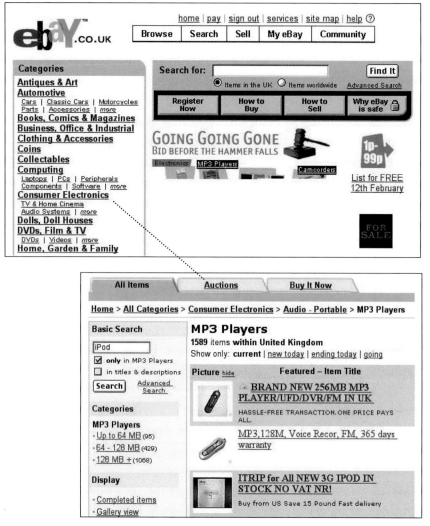

I could list category after category of things that are available on eBay, but we'd be here all day and all you really have to do is look through the categories list to get a rough idea.

Clicking on any of these categories will take you to subdivisions of the categories. After the headings for these, you will find (in brackets) how many items appear in each subcategory. For instance, let's say I'm after some Royal Doulton china. In the category 'Pottery, Porcelain & Glass' I type in 'Royal

Doulton'. There are 5,514 items. I want a 'Winnie The Pooh' figure. I can click on the subcategory 'animals' on the left of figure 2, then either browse through all 163 items, or set up another search, within the Royal Doulton 'animals' subcategory.

Fig 2. Item listings from category links

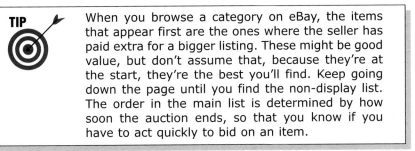

When I do this, I find just three Pooh items on sale. Click on the item description and I'm taken to the full listing for the item. But there are 7,935 Pooh items on eBay as I type. I don't want to read them all, but by sticking to the narrow category where they ought to be, I've eliminated too many. So I type 'Winnie The Pooh Royal Doulton' into a general search box. I get 103 hits. The other Pooh items are in subcategories like 'seriesware'. I also get hits under 'collectables'. The moral? Unless you're certain that all sellers will use the same categories as you, use a general search first.

> **TIP**
>
> When you browse a category on eBay, the items that appear first are the ones where the seller has paid extra for a bigger listing. These might be good value, but don't assume that, because they're at the start, they're the best you'll find. Keep going down the page until you find the non-display list. The order in the main list is determined by how soon the auction ends, so that you know if you have to act quickly to bid on an item.

You now have enough information to go browsing on eBay, where you can find anything, from a running machine to keep you fit, through to a long-unavailable Barbie doll to delight your daughter or granddaughter. But remember, until you've registered, you can't bid. We'll look at registration in the next section.

What do I have to do to register?

Registration takes a couple of minutes. You don't need to give credit card details unless you want to start selling at once (or if you're using an anonymous web-based email account like Hotmail or Yahoo, when a card number is required to verify you are who you say you are and confirm your address – most sellers won't send goods to a buyer who doesn't have a confirmed address). You'll be asked to fill in a form like the one below.

User ID

The most time-consuming part of the registration process is choosing your User ID and password. eBay doesn't allow you to use your email address as your User ID. Any User ID will do provided it isn't obscene, very silly or (much more likely) already taken by another eBayer. If your first choice is already in use, a screen will pop up and ask you to choose something else. You can change your User ID later, if you really need to, so don't tear your hair out over the decision. Sellers don't tend to refuse buyers because they don't like their name, and vice versa.

Fig 3. Registering on eBay for the first time

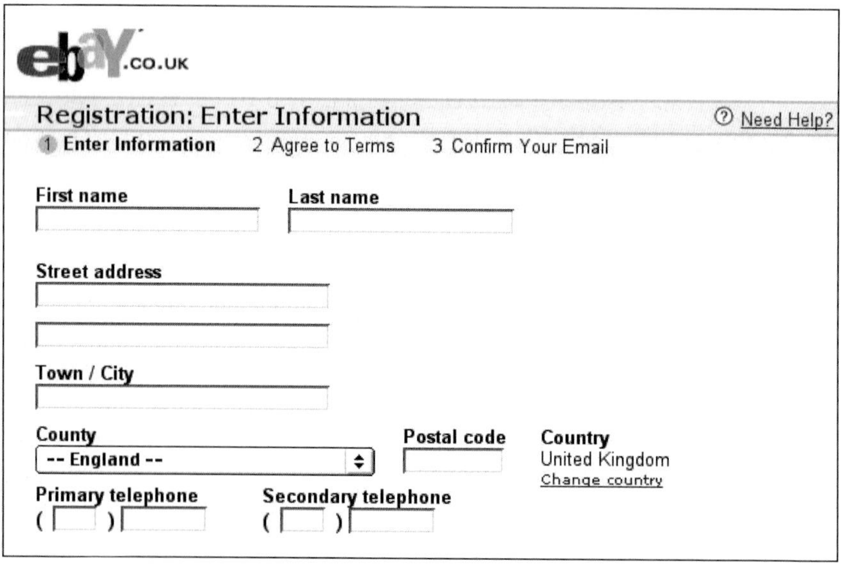

eb**aY**.co.uk

Registration: Enter Information   ⑦ Need Help?

① Enter Information   2 Agree to Terms   3 Confirm Your Email

First name   Last name

Street address

Town / City

County   Postal code   Country
-- England --   United Kingdom
                                                    Change country

Primary telephone   Secondary telephone
(   )   (   )

If you haven't got a second phone number, don't worry. Leave this box blank. You have to fill in all the other information.

Fig 3. cont

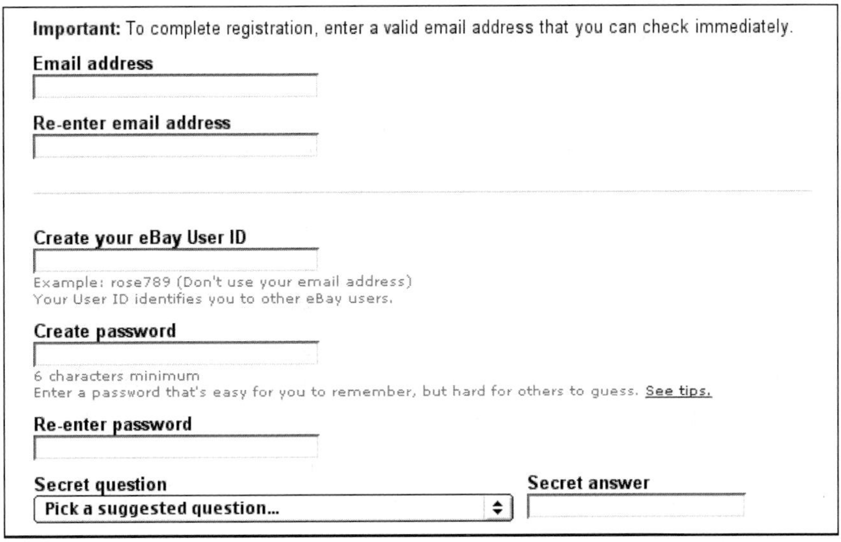

Important: To complete registration, enter a valid email address that you can check immediately.

Email address

Re-enter email address

Create your eBay User ID

Example: rose789 (Don't use your email address)
Your User ID identifies you to other eBay users.

Create password

6 characters minimum
Enter a password that's easy for you to remember, but hard for others to guess. <u>See tips.</u>

Re-enter password

Secret question

Pick a suggested question...

Secret answer

Password

For your password, choose a different word, or combination of letters and numbers, from your User ID – one that you will find easy to remember.

eBay makes heavy use of 'cookies' (hidden bits of code that tell a site who the visitor is) so that, once you've registered, it will recognise you when you come back and you won't have to type in your password every time you want to use a personalised part of the eBay site. That said, eBay will still ask for your password quite frequently. This is because use of the password prevents other people using your account on your computer. For added security, you will also be asked to provide a security question (e.g. your mother's maiden name) and your date of birth.

The contact information you provide when registering will not be passed on by eBay to anyone else. The company has a strict privacy policy, and European law prevents it from selling your name to junk mailers or email spammers even if it wanted to do so. However, buyers or sellers can get hold of your contact details if they have a legitimate reason to get in touch with you, i.e. when, for whatever reason, they're unable to contact you by email.

Sometimes when you register, you will be invited to complete an eBay survey. You might be asked how you heard about eBay and other marketing questions. You can complete the survey if you want to, but it's not obligatory, and if you don't want to you can simply close the window without being disadvantaged in any way.

Email confirmation

Within a few minutes of submitting your registration, you'll get an email from eBay. It will give you a registration code, and ask you to click a button labelled 'Complete eBay Registration'. Doing this confirms to eBay that your email address is valid, and as soon as you do it, you can start to bid on auctions.

Next to the register button on the eBay homepage, you'll see buttons labelled 'how to sell' and 'how to buy', plus another called 'why eBay is safe'. Read these if you feel like it, or stick with this book for the time being and go searching for something you'd like to bid on (but don't bid until you've read the next section).

Using bookmarks

I'd suggest bookmarking the main eBay.co.uk page. Now click on the link to the eBay site map and bookmark that page too. (In Internet Explorer you do this by clicking on the 'Favourites' menu, then clicking on 'Add page to favourites'). You'll need both later.

If you find yourself using eBay regularly, you'll want to set up a folder of eBay bookmarks (Some browsers automatically configure an 'Auction favourites' folder). This is easily done by going into the 'Favourites' menu and clicking on 'Organise favourites.' You can bookmark all of your favourite or most used eBay pages. After a while, the ones you'll probably use most are your favourite searches and the 'My eBay' page.

Most pages have a search button like the one near the top right of the site map. Once you start bidding, eBay will automatically set up your 'My eBay' page for you. For the moment, it's simplest to stick with the eBay homepage. So use the bookmark you've just set or press your browser's 'back' button and return there.

Building up feedback

Unusually, for reasons explained in the introduction, I was an eBay seller before I bought anything. For most eBayers, it makes more sense to buy first. That way, you learn how the system works and can also build up positive feedback. Feedback is the peer rating system that is crucial to how eBay works. In theory, after every transaction, both buyer and seller leave feedback about how the deal went. The theory doesn't always work, for reasons we'll come to. For the most part,

> "For most eBayers, it makes more sense to buy first. That way, you learn how the system works and can also build up positive feedback."

though, feedback is a reliable guide to how smoothly a transaction is likely to go if you buy from, or sell to, the party concerned.

Many buyers won't deal with sellers who have a tiny feedback score, so it makes sense to do some buying and get a few positive feedback points first. If you only want to sell, as I did at first, feedback isn't essential, but you may end up getting fewer bids and a lower price than a seasoned seller would.

Most sellers will accept a buyer with no feedback. (Everybody had to start from nowhere once.) Occasionally, a seller might exclude them, or refuse to post goods until a cheque has cleared (many do this to everybody, routinely). If either of these things happens, don't object. There are plenty of scammers out there and new users cause a disproportionately large amount of payment problems, so it's reasonable for sellers to protect themselves.

Searching

Searching by using the search box

There are two basic ways to search eBay. The most straightforward is to use the simple box that appears at the top of most eBay pages and treat it like a search engine. In some browsers, a predictive search box will appear, showing recent items you've searched on to save you typing them in again (there's also an advanced search, which we'll come to). To begin with, stick with searching items listed in the UK, checking the box as in the following illustration.

Fig 4. Search options box

This will give you fewer items to look through than a worldwide search. Other reasons for sticking to UK items at first are that the security risk is lower (it's not easy to chase a defaulting seller in Iowa) and postage is quicker and cheaper.

The other basic search box you will see is shown below. It gives you the option of searching either against the auction title only, or against both the title and the item description.

Fig 5. Search box

Leave this box unticked if you just want the search to be done against the auction's title.

Tick it if you want the search to be done against the item's description too (will yield more results)

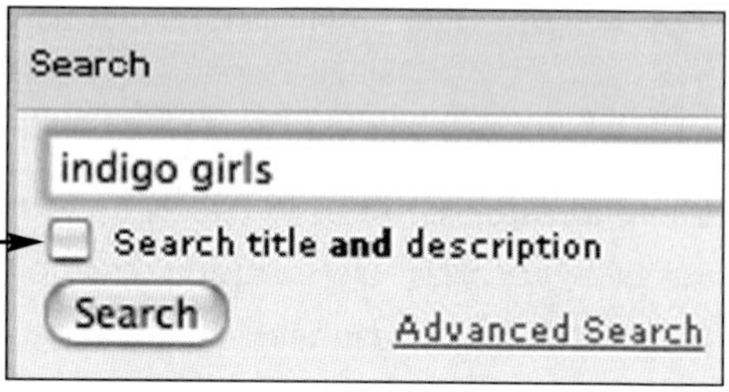

After a while, you'll learn which items it's worth searching in descriptions for. Usually, putting a tick in the 'in titles and descriptions' box will give you a longer list containing things that you aren't looking for. But in some categories the ability to do a more detailed search can be helpful. At one end of the spectrum, this might be a particularly specific type of collectable, at the other some more ordinary item that you've discovered is often misdescribed.

Searching by using the category list

The other way to search is to use the category list on the left of the homepage (you can see the start of the list in fig 1. on page 24). This is slower, and more akin to window shopping. If you restrict yourself to UK-based items, the number of items will be lower and the list correspondingly shorter, which means that you may be able to search through an entire category, even if you're still using a dial-up modem. One disadvantage of a category search, though, is that it will miss out a lot of items that are not listed in the right category. For instance, when I look in the 'fridge magnets' category, I get 149 items. When I put the key words 'fridge magnet' into the search box, I get more than 4,000. Most items are categorised according to what picture is on the magnet, making a category search useless.

> **TIP**
>
> Here's a tip that took me years to discover: if you decide to look at any of the items listed, hold down the capitals key, second up on the left (or the Apple key if you use a Mac) when you click on it. That way, a new window opens and you keep the old page open beneath it. Whichever page you click on will be highlighted. By reading one page while waiting for another to load, you save loads of time (the Firefox browser has a clever cache system that allows you to flick between pages in just one window).

There are almost as many entries (3,740 items) for 'Music and Concerts' (not including records, tapes or cds). That's too many to go through. You can click on the link and see the auctions that are about to end soon. But if you're after something specific – say, good seats for a sold-out show by Elton John – your best bet is to go to the search box that appears on the left of the Music and Concerts page. First, put a tick on the box that says 'search only in Music and Concert'. Then type in the words 'Elton John' (to narrow down the search further, add the word 'tickets' and the name of the city where you want to see him).

I used to browse the general categories when I started out, but I soon learnt to search eBay only for fairly specific things, by putting the key words into my search and using quotation marks in the search to match a precise phrase. Using quotation marks is a useful tip in any kind of search. They tell the search engine to locate the right words in the right order, considerably narrowing down the number of results you have to sift through. I find this time-efficient, but everybody uses eBay in different ways. Browsing will turn up things you didn't know you wanted and ones where the seller has made a spelling mistake (which can lead to bargains). Over time, you'll find the techniques and short cuts that suit your style. Using this book should allow you to make that transition more quickly and smoothly. We've only scratched the surface of using search tools and we'll come back to them later. In the next section, we'll look at how to start buying.

Buying on eBay

New eBay users often make the same mistake as Philip on page 9. They think they're involved in a 'live' auction, not understanding how the proxy bidding system works. There are situations in eBay auctions where you really do go head-to-head with someone else. We'll come to those at the end of this section, which takes you step by step through the process of buying on eBay.co.uk.

Check feedback before bidding

Before bidding, check that the item you're thinking of bidding on is exactly what you want and in a condition you find acceptable. If there isn't enough detail about the item, you can email the seller a question (if they don't reply, don't bid). Once you're sure about that, check that the seller has decent feedback.

Fig 6. Checking the seller's feedback

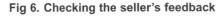

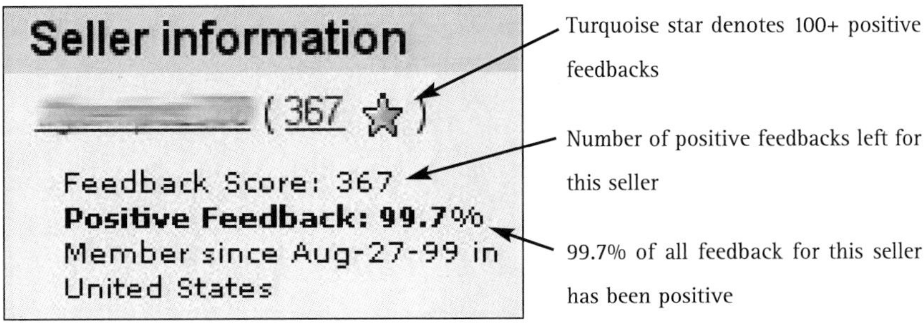

Seller information

_____ (367 ☆)

Feedback Score: 367
Positive Feedback: 99.7%
Member since Aug-27-99 in United States

Turquoise star denotes 100+ positive feedbacks

Number of positive feedbacks left for this seller

99.7% of all feedback for this seller has been positive

If you click on a seller's feedback score (the underlined blue '367' in fig 6.), you'll be taken to the seller's feedback profile, where you find a complete record of their history on eBay. This particular seller has just one, quite recent, negative amongst the otherwise glowing feedback reports. It reads like this: "Very disappointed, poorly packed, arrived broken." The seller is allowed to reply to the buyer's negative feedback. In this case, they have written: "Packed securely, surprised it broke, insured item, comment unfair, resolvable."

I'd certainly buy an item from the seller above. However, I'd be very dubious about dealing with anyone whose feedback is lower than 98%. If in doubt, read through the feedback until you find the negatives (or do a negative-only search, see page 66). Often the seller has a convincing explanation like the one above. If the seller trades insults, or leaves the negative comment unchallenged, think very carefully before bidding.

TIP

If somebody sells a lot, then, with the best will in the world, they're liable to get some negative feedback. We all make mistakes and there are people who are never satisfied, or like making trouble, or are trying to perpetrate some kind of fraud themselves. Bear in mind that on eBay it's easy to bid in haste and repent at leisure.

Fools rush in

Never bid on an item as soon as you see it. Check out what else is on offer first. It's very rare that a genuinely 'one-off' item shows up on eBay. A couple of years ago, flush with money in my PayPal account, I got into a bidding war over an obscure early EP featuring one of my favourite singers, Aimee Mann. I won it for what I believed was a reasonable price, albeit more than I had ever paid in an auction before. A week after I won, a pristine copy of the same EP came up on eBay. It sold for less than half the price I'd paid, probably to the person who was runner-up in the auction I won. Lesson learnt.

Bidding for the first time

You've looked around, found something you want and are ready to put a toe in the water. What should you think about before getting wet? As with a live auction, it is sensible to decide the maximum you are prepared to pay for an item before you start bidding. Keep it on the low side to begin with. The item's likely to come up again and you can raise your bid if you get outbid. Go to the bottom left of the screen and find out what the starting bid is. If you're bidding on a non-UK auction, make sure that the seller will post the item to the UK. Always check the postage and packing details, along with the payment methods, to make sure that they're acceptable to you (more on this, and customs issues, later). Here are two examples:

Fig 7. Seller's postage & payment requirements – 1

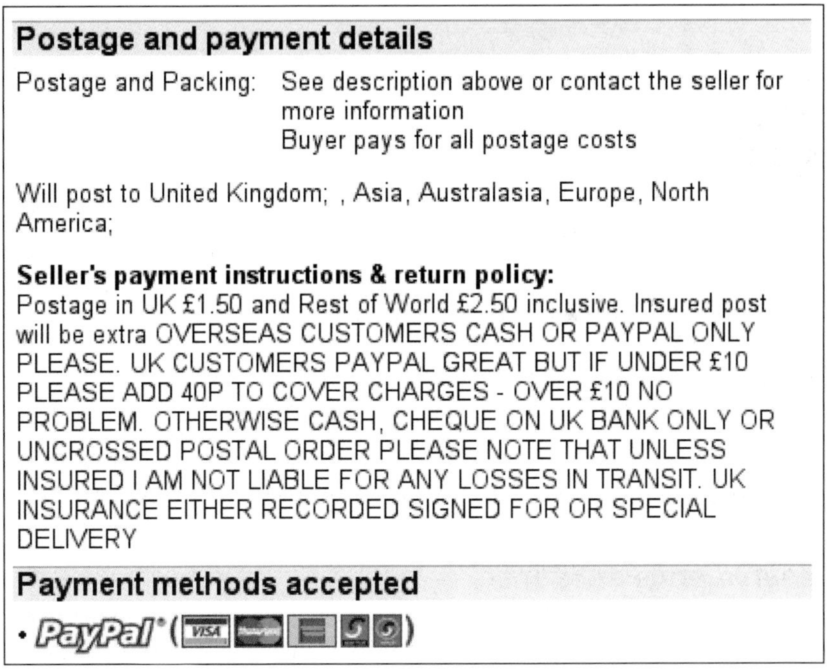

Postage and payment details

Postage and Packing: See description above or contact the seller for
more information
Buyer pays for all postage costs

Will post to United Kingdom; , Asia, Australasia, Europe, North America;

Seller's payment instructions & return policy:
Postage in UK £1.50 and Rest of World £2.50 inclusive. Insured post will be extra OVERSEAS CUSTOMERS CASH OR PAYPAL ONLY PLEASE. UK CUSTOMERS PAYPAL GREAT BUT IF UNDER £10 PLEASE ADD 40P TO COVER CHARGES - OVER £10 NO PROBLEM. OTHERWISE CASH, CHEQUE ON UK BANK ONLY OR UNCROSSED POSTAL ORDER PLEASE NOTE THAT UNLESS INSURED I AM NOT LIABLE FOR ANY LOSSES IN TRANSIT. UK INSURANCE EITHER RECORDED SIGNED FOR OR SPECIAL DELIVERY

Payment methods accepted

• PayPal (VISA)

Fig 8. Seller's postage & payment requirements - 2

Shipping and handling: Free Shipping (within United States)

Will ship to United States only.

Seller's payment instructions & return policy:
Let me know if you want insurance. All sales final. Thanks!

Payment methods accepted

• **PayPal** (VISA · · · ECHECK eBay)
• Personal check
• Money order/Cashiers check
Learn about payment methods.

Ready to bid?

LOVE AND ROCKETS #1 Self-Published Comic B/W

Starting bid: US $55.00

Your maximum bid: **US $** [   ] (Enter **US $55.00** or more)

[**Place Bid >**]

eBay automatically bids on your behalf **up to** your maximum bid.
Learn about bidding.

In the UK, you'd be fine with the seller in fig 7. One of his charges – the 40p surcharge for PayPal – is now against eBay rules but wasn't when he listed. But you wouldn't be OK with the seller in fig 8. There would be no point in bidding on the auction in fig 8. because the seller will only post to the United States. If you bid on and win the comic in the auction, you risk getting negative feedback. The seller might agree to sell it to you, but would be entitled to refuse (because you broke the terms of the auction), sell it to the next highest bidder and leave you negative feedback for your mistake.

Reserve price auctions

Sometimes, a seller sets a reserve, just like in real-life auctions. However, reserves tend to be used sparingly, as their presence tends to put buyers off. In a reserve price listing, the listing fee is based on the reserve price for your item, not the starting bid. There is also an additional reserve price listing fee, which is refunded if your item sells – see pages 163-167 for details.

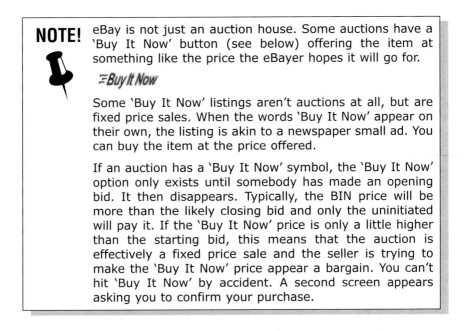

NOTE! eBay is not just an auction house. Some auctions have a 'Buy It Now' button (see below) offering the item at something like the price the eBayer hopes it will go for.

≡Buy It Now

Some 'Buy It Now' listings aren't auctions at all, but are fixed price sales. When the words 'Buy It Now' appear on their own, the listing is akin to a newspaper small ad. You can buy the item at the price offered.

If an auction has a 'Buy It Now' symbol, the 'Buy It Now' option only exists until somebody has made an opening bid. It then disappears. Typically, the BIN price will be more than the likely closing bid and only the uninitiated will pay it. If the 'Buy It Now' price is only a little higher than the starting bid, this means that the auction is effectively a fixed price sale and the seller is trying to make the 'Buy It Now' price appear a bargain. You can't hit 'Buy It Now' by accident. A second screen appears asking you to confirm your purchase.

Time to bid - a summary

You've checked the item description carefully and it's what you want, in the condition you require, from a seller who appears reliable. The postage and packing charge is acceptable and the seller is willing to deliver it to where you live. The starting bid is low enough for you to think you have a chance of winning at a price you're willing to pay. OK, scroll down to the box at the bottom left of the page, which looks like this:

Fig 9. Placing a bid

(At the time of writing, the 'place bid' button appears at the top of the page as well, but if you use the top button, you have to go to a new page to state the amount of your maximum bid.)

Choose your maximum bid. This should be the most you're willing to pay, bearing in mind that there may well be other copies of the same item on offer. In the illustration in fig 8, as you're the first bidder on this outstanding paperback novel, you're bound to be the highest bidder. I wouldn't place too high a bid though. I happen to know that, although the title is out of print, there are about 40,000 copies in circulation in the UK alone. A fraction over two quid should secure it, unless an unusually keen bidder comes along.

What happens next

eBay will take you to a page where it asks you to review and confirm your bid (you will have to sign in, using your password, if you haven't done so already in your current eBay browsing session). When you have confirmed your bid, it will either take you to a page telling you that 'congratulations, you are the current high bidder' or 'sorry, you've been outbid'. If you are the high bidder, you will also be sent an email telling you this. eBay will also send you an email if you are outbid later in the auction, giving you the opportunity to re-enter the auction with a higher bid of your own.

If you win

If you win the auction, eBay will send you an email. This will tell you the seller's payment instructions. You can follow these straight away. (If you're watching the auction as it happens, you can also follow the payment instructions from the auction page itself.) You don't have to wait for the seller to contact you. If you have a PayPal account (see the PayPal section on page 121), you can often deal with the matter in a few clicks, not even having to type out your address or keep a copy of the seller's address. But most sellers in the UK will accept postal orders, a cheque or even well-concealed cash (at the sender's risk).

Good communication is what makes eBay work well, so if you're posting the seller payment for the goods, it's wise to use eBay's 'send a message to the seller' box to tell them this. Bear in mind that, if sending a personal cheque, the seller may wait until your cheque has cleared before sending the goods. After all, at this stage, you don't have any feedback to convince the seller that you're a trustworthy person. When the item arrives, if everything has gone as advertised you should leave positive feedback for the seller and they, hopefully, will do the same. Guidance on leaving feedback is covered in section 4, 'Feedback', starting on page 61.

> "Good communication is what makes eBay work well."

You've been outbid

Let's go back a step or two. You've made your first bid. Maybe you got lucky and won first time out. More likely, you were cautious and have already been outbid, by proxy, and are trying to decide whether to bid again. It's tempting to get carried away, especially if the auction is about to end. Before you bid again, here are a couple of things to think about.

- Do you really want the item?
- Is it likely that more examples of the item will show up on eBay shortly? (You might be able to get it more cheaply when there are fewer bidders.)

  You *still* want it?

- OK, what's the real maximum that you're willing to spend? Before you bid this maximum, why don't you check that you can't find the item online at a price cheaper than that?

  You can't?

- OK, bid again and follow the advice in the previous section.

Sniping

The big difference between an eBay auction and one in a regular auction house is not that the bidders can be anywhere in the world. It's that **the auction has to end at a certain time.** Listings can be set for 1, 3, 5, 7 or 10 days. Some auctions are effectively over within a day or two, because the people interested in the item have competed over it until one dropped out. But you never know, somebody with deeper pockets may come along in the last few minutes. They may even bid in the closing seconds, so as not to allow the former winning bid time to raise his or her maximum bid.

In many eBay auctions (not the majority, but a fairly high proportion) the winning bid is made in the last minute or two. This is called 'sniping' and is discussed again later on in this book. For now, though, a word of basic advice. *You'll only lose out to a sniper if you're a cheapskate.* If your maximum bid is what the item is worth to you, then a last-minute bidder can only beat your bid by paying *more* than the item is worth to you.

By bidding late, the 'sniper' hopes to keep other buyers ignorant of his or her interest and thereby keep the price low. More importantly, by going just over your maximum bid and not giving you time to respond, the sniper hopes to avoid a bidding war and get the item for less than they would in a conventional auction. This hurts

> "In many eBay auctions the winning bid is made in the last minute or two."

the seller, who may not get as much as they would have done in a real-life auction. But it only hurts the losing bidder if they've bid less than they're willing to pay.

NOTE! If you follow an auction live, keeping a couple of browser windows open and refreshing the page every 10 seconds, sniping and being sniped can make for a pretty exciting end to an auction. Broadband helps, and you should consider using automated sniping tools, as other bidders often will.

Sniping is a perfectly legitimate bidding tactic.

The thrill of the chase

Last year I was chasing a DVD of the US movie 'Lost In Translation'. At the time, the film was still showing in UK cinemas. In the USA, it had come out on DVD a few days previously. I typed the title and 'DVD' into the search box near the top right-hand corner of the page, then clicked on 'find it' to see what showed up a few seconds later. I'd already bid on one copy, but didn't win it. I could have done a global search and got more to choose from, but I wanted the DVD quickly so I restricted my search to the UK. Also, for reasons I'll go into later, many US sellers won't sell outside their own country. I could have probably tracked down a cheap copy in Malaysia, but it would almost certainly have been a fake. Pirate discs are often precise clones of the real thing, if you excuse the odd spelling mistake on the cover, but I don't buy them.

There were eight copies on offer. I bid on the auction that ended soonest, making sure that the DVD was in widescreen and that the seller had a 100% feedback record. I set my maximum bid at £12.49. The seller only charges 60p postage, the actual cost of the stamps. (I used to charge actual postage, but now I add a bit, to cover the time I spend wrapping things carefully and cycling to the Post Office.) I didn't think I'd win the auction. The DVD was too new, too in demand and the copy I bid on the previous day went for £14.50 (plus £1.50 postage). But you never know – it was a 'region one' DVD and many people don't have the multi-region players that allow you to play coded discs intended for an area other than the one you're in. If I didn't get it this time, there were seven more on sale. I logged a couple of the more promising ones on my eBay watching page so that I could find another one later if I was outbid. The auction I bid on ended in fifteen hours.

eBay always emails you to confirm that you're the current high bidder. It also emails you if you get outbid. I got an outbid notice for the 'Lost In Translation' DVD a couple of hours after I bid on it. The top bid was £12.99 and stayed there. The successful buyer would have got the DVD for just 40p less than the cost of a new copy on the net (taking into account postage costs), so it wasn't worth my bidding higher. This, I suspect my old Economics A-level teacher would have told me, is an example of a free and open market setting a fair price.

Still keen to get a DVD of 'Lost In Translation', I checked my eBay watching page. There was one more copy of the DVD in an auction that ended the next day, so I clicked on it. There was a day of the auction left and the price was £10.65. I checked how much the seller was charging for postage: £2 – a rip-off. If I won at the next bid increment, I'd only save a few pence on the new price. So I left it. The final price was £11.15. Once you add the postage, that's virtually the same price as the other one.

A couple of days later, I spotted another copy that was due to end soon. The postage was a rip-off but the price was quite low, so I made a bid. It wasn't high enough.

Fig 10. 'You have been outbid' message

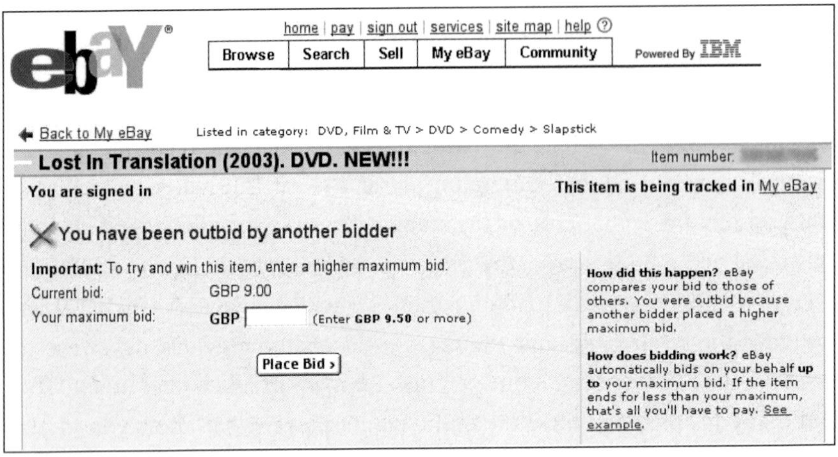

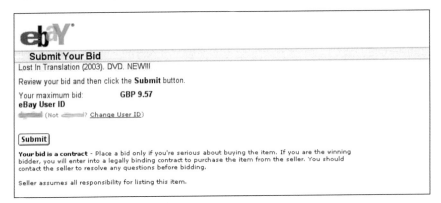

The price was still quite a lot lower than the fourteen quid it would've cost me elsewhere, so I had another go, this time bidding a maximum of £9.57.

Fig 11. Increasing a maximum bid in response to an outbid

This too resulted in a 'You have been outbid' message. I had one more go, increasing my maximum bid to £11.02, where my saving would be a mere 97p. The result? I was the high bidder at £10.79, as the screenshot opposite shows.

Fig 12. Current high bidder!

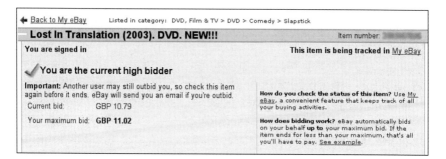

Just before the auction ended, however, I got this email:

Fig 13. Outbid again . . .

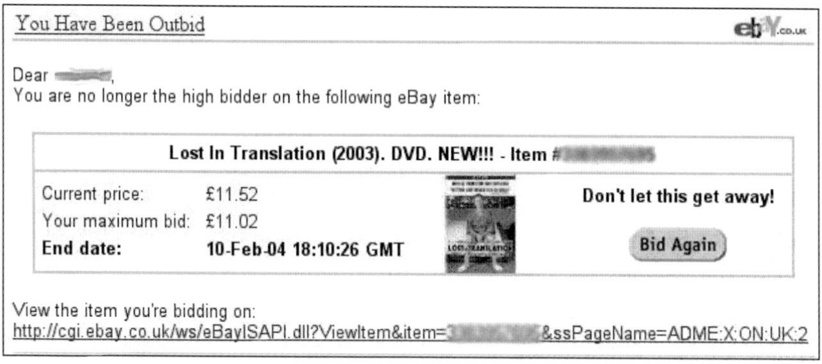

I could've pressed the 'bid again' button, but it wasn't worth it to me. As it turned out, I'd have been wasting my time. The final price of this copy of the film was £12.50 (plus £2 post and packing). The price was going up.

I should have learnt by now that one of the things not worth buying on eBay are popular new releases of any kind. I'd already seen this movie at a cinema. People who haven't are willing to pay a premium price to watch it in the comfort of their own homes. After a few months, it was much easier to find a cheap copy. As it is, by combining shipping with another item, I managed to get the DVD from the US Amazon site for a fraction under thirteen pounds, including postage – a bargain, as long as Customs didn't decide to charge VAT on my purchase. Another lesson: eBay isn't always the cheapest place to shop, especially when the dollar is low.

Using 'My eBay' and more essential buying tips

● ●

What not to buy

For some people, eBay is the first stop for almost everything they want to buy that can't be eaten or drunk. And why not? If you can get whatever you're after at a good price without leaving home, it makes sense to do so. Browsing eBay auctions with some mp3s or an online radio station playing in the background is more relaxing than going to the shops (though you're less likely to bump into people you know). You might find it addictive.

But are there things you shouldn't buy on eBay? Too many to list. There are no hard-and-fast rules about which products are safe and which are risky, but the following general principles will keep you out of trouble.

✗
- ✗ Don't buy anything that **doesn't travel well** (i.e. perishable or very fragile items) unless the seller makes clear how it will reach you safely.
- ✗ Don't buy anything where the **postage cost** vastly exceeds the value of the item (unless, of course, you really, really want it).
- ✗ Don't buy goods that are **illegal** to sell on eBay. You will have no comeback if the goods turn out to be faulty or counterfeit.
- ✗ Don't buy **autographs** or other **memorabilia** items unless their authentication is a hundred and ten percent.

Who not to buy from

- Don't buy from sellers with poor feedback or who provide dodgy descriptions of their items.

- Don't buy from sellers who don't respond to emailed queries.

- Be very careful about bidding on pricey items from new sellers who have unusually high positive feedback for selling much cheaper items. They may have used dubious means to build up their feedback before pulling off an expensive scam.

- Be wary of sellers with a recently changed User ID (this used to be indicated by a rather appropriate symbol showing a pair of sunglasses 👓 next to the User ID, but now looks like this):

The seller may have a legitimate reason for changing ID, but may be trying to hide from past customers who they've given a bad deal.

New users

If the seller has a logo like this – 👤 – it means that they're a new user, registered in the last thirty days or so. The same logo will appear next to your name in your first month if you're shown as the high bidder on an item. New users will have low (or even no) feedback. There's no reason not to bid on their auctions if everything else looks right, but you should exercise caution and cut the seller a little slack at the end of the transaction if they're not completely confident in dealing with you (they might not have read this book, after all).

Prohibited, questionable and infringing items

eBay prohibits all sorts of items, some of which still slip through the net and get listed. If you buy one, you have less protection from eBay than with permitted items. You can see a list of the banned categories on the eBay site map, titled 'Prohibited, questionable and infringing items'. Below are some examples.

Partial list of prohibited, questionable and infringing items

- used underwear (or any clothing that hasn't been washed)
- airline tickets
- material with sexual and erotic content
- alcohol
- drugs
- animals
- plants
- seeds
- lock-picking devices
- football tickets

If you're wondering why some of these appear on the P,Q & I list, look at the full list on eBay. There are explanations for all the outlawed items. eBay also bans auctioning any kind of downloads, unless you specifically state that you own the copyright (although this does not stop such auctions appearing – if reported, they should be taken down) and selling CD-Rs or DVD-Rs, unless they're blank. Copyright is, and should be, a big issue on eBay.

✔ Caution

eBay advises extreme caution when buying some other things. Autographs, for instance, are always questionable, even when accompanied by a so-called certificate of authenticity. Arguably, you shouldn't buy an autographed item unless you have a photograph of the item in question actually being signed by the person whose autograph it is. But that would rule out most legitimate autographs, a point which leads me to another tip.

Badly described items can be worth the risk

In 2003 I bought some early (mid-80s) issues of my favourite ever independent comic book – 'Love And Rockets' by the Hernandez Brothers – ones that came out back when there were three of them. The seller said they were signed but offered no authentication. I was more concerned that they were first editions. The seller didn't say so, but I guessed they were. As it turned out, all but one were first editions. And all five comics were signed. Each of the three brothers had signed their own individual stories in each comic. I was able to check the signatures against my signed copy of the first ever issue of 'Love And Rockets'. They were undoubtedly genuine. The comics were in better condition than advertised too, almost perfect. A bargain.

There are bargains to be had all over eBay and sometimes, to get lucky, you have to take a risk. I could have emailed this particular seller, asking very specific questions. Had I done so, I might easily have alerted him to the fact that the comics were worth far more than the starting bid I ended up getting them for. It's easy for a seller to end an auction early especially if there have been no bids. Sometimes, a certain amount of tactical cunning is called for on the buyer's part.

'My eBay'

There are other buying habits that are worth getting into early on. When you look at an item, you'll see a button called 'Watch this item in My eBay'. If you want to keep an eye on the auction, click the button to add it to your 'My eBay' page. If you ask the seller a question, you will automatically be offered the chance to add the auction to your watch list. 'My eBay' is the watching page that eBay will automatically set up for you once you're registered and have started bidding or selling. It links to pages for selling, buying and favourite searches. This is the page you might well make your eBay 'homepage' (note – because it has

'You can watch up to thirty items on your My eBay page.'

to search for information about you, it takes longer to load than the real eBay homepage or site map).

Your 'My eBay' page allows you to keep track of auctions you're bidding on and auctions you're watching. You can watch up to thirty items on your My eBay page. You can even watch up to ten items as a guest if you haven't got round to registering yet. The page illustrated in fig 14. over the page will also show you items you've won and haven't won during a time period of your choice. It lists items you've bid on but failed to win. Items that you're watching stay on the list until you delete them, which is useful if you want to compare prices when a new item comes up.

Also shown overleaf in fig 16. is the top half of my 'watching' page. Where there's no number in the 'number of bids' column and the auction has ended, as these all have, it means that the item failed to sell. Keeping a watch on the price that an item you're about to sell goes for is a useful thing to do when you become a seller. You can remove items from your watch list at any time by ticking the boxes on the left of the screen, scrolling down, and clicking the 'delete' button.

By clicking on the 'selling' tab on fig 14. you can see the current state of all the auctions you're running (this has an extra feature, allowing you to see how many people are currently 'watching' your auction). You can set up a 'favourites' page by clicking on that link, giving you a quick route to your favourite stores or sellers, your favourite categories and most used searches.

If, after you've done a search, you click on 'Add to My Favourite Searches', this page will allow you to repeat searches without having to type the criteria in all over again. This is especially useful when you move on to advanced searches. If you want, eBay will even email you every time a new item appears that matches your search. You should only select this option for the more obscure items, or you'll get swamped.

Fig 14. Top part of the 'My eBay' page

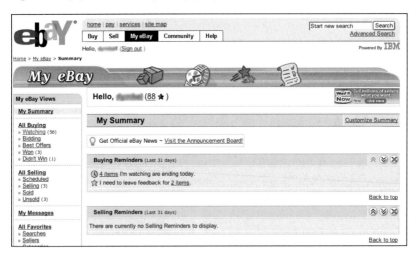

Fig 15. Compare items feature

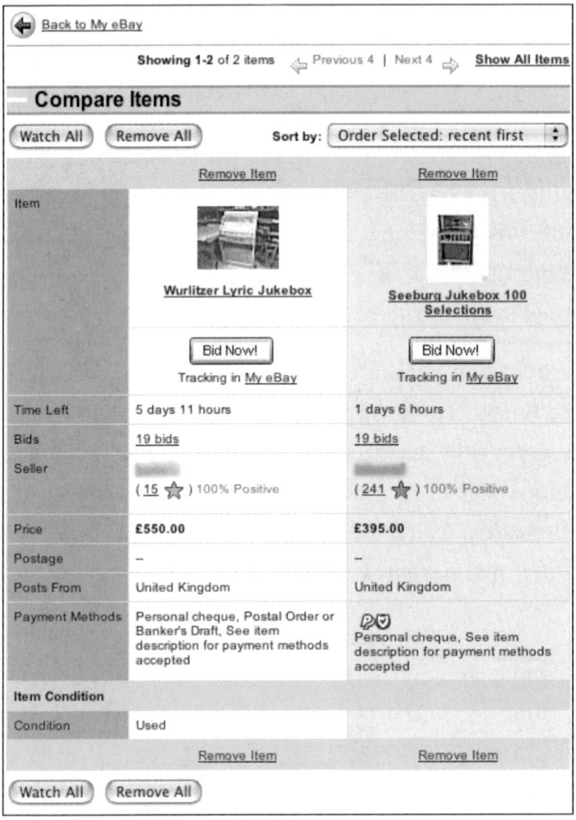

Fig 16. 'Items I'm Watching' part of the 'My eBay' page

Check boxes of the items you no longer want to watch, and click the 'delete' button. When the page refreshes, they will be gone.

By ticking two of the buttons on the left, then clicking on 'compare', you can see the basics of two items side by side, to aid comparison. (See Fig 15.)

By clicking on 'add note' you are able to add information (see the Springsteen ticket third down) to jog your memory.

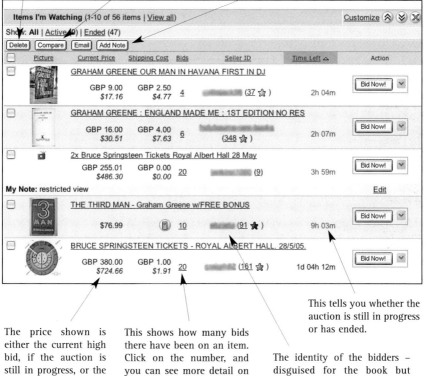

The price shown is either the current high bid, if the auction is still in progress, or the final bid, if the auction has ended.

This shows how many bids there have been on an item. Click on the number, and you can see more detail on the bidding.

This tells you whether the auction is still in progress or has ended.

The identity of the bidders – disguised for the book but online you'd be able to see who they are. Click on their names and see their feedback.

Advanced searches

Browsing can be an enjoyable way to pass a spare half hour but is rarely the best way to find a specific item. 'Normal' searches can throw up more results than you have time go through, especially if you don't have a fast internet connection. Sooner, rather than later, you'll probably want to use the advanced search page, which looks like this when you click on it:

Fig 17. Advanced search page

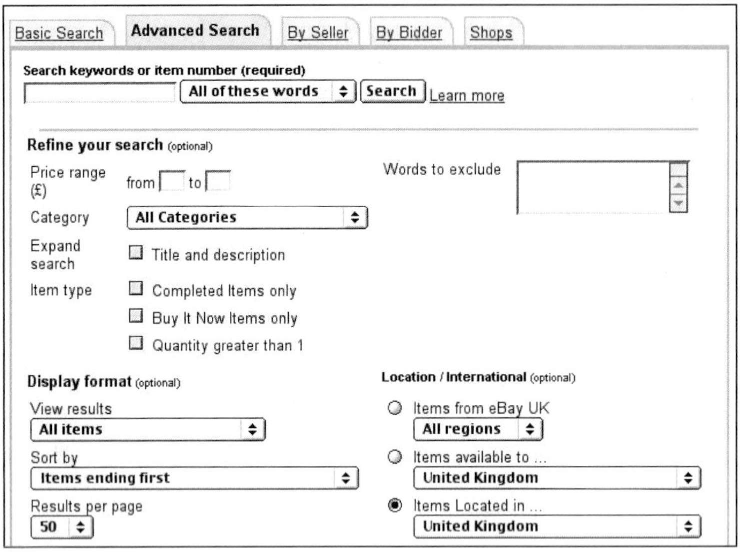

The 'Search keywords' option allows you to specify that you want an exact phrase (putting your keywords in "quotation marks" in the ordinary search box has the same effect). So, for instance, if I'm looking for a book I haven't read by the writer Laurie Hulse Anderson, putting her name in quotation marks will stop me accidentally getting lots of search results for the performing artist Laurie Anderson. Putting the names of the books I don't want in the 'words to exclude' box will narrow it down further.

The 'Completed items only' box is of use if you're a seller looking to find how much an item has gone for recently, or a buyer, wanting to make sure you don't pay too much. It limits your search to auctions that have finished and which resulted in a sale, thus giving an indication of realised values.

The price range search can be a useful way of sifting out underpriced items (likely to be of poor quality) or overpriced items (more than you want to pay). The 'words to exclude' option is another good way of containing the number of search results. You might, for example, do a search for a certain type of doll but want to exclude the more common categories, so putting the words 'Cinderella' or 'Barbie' in the exclude box would usefully restrict the search. There are other more sophisticated ways of searching, not all of which I have room to go into here. Take a look at:

- search.ebay.co.uk/ws/search/SearchCustomization

for more info. Another useful tip is to use the '+' key in the search box, to narrow down a search. So, for instance, say you want to buy a ticket to see the REM tour that's going on as I write, but only want a standing ticket, you could type REM, Sheffield +standing and only results that included standing tickets would appear. Putting double quotation marks around a phrase will only bring up auctions including that exact phrase. Putting a '*' immediately after the search string will bring up variables of that word.

'Buy It Now' searches are useful if you want something in a hurry, although you should probably do a sort by 'items ending first' before trying. That may throw up normal auctions which are about to end, and, as previously noted, you are more likely to get a bargain on a normal auction than on a 'Buy It Now' purchase.

If you do the same search frequently, or want to find 'Buy It Now' bargains before somebody else does, the 'sort by newly listed items first' is worth a go. Another useful tip: if you find that you often look at a particular seller's auctions, it can be worth clicking on the 'View seller's other auctions' link on the item description page. There are a couple of sellers who I keep bookmarked because they often have items I'm interested in.

Location, location, location

You'll see that on the screenshot opposite there are three location buttons. The one that I'd be most inclined to highlight is 'Items available to United Kingdom'. This saves you sorting through all the US items where the seller, for whatever reason, refuses to sell overseas. The UK regions section is only really of use if you're after something where it makes sense to collect the item rather than post it, like, for example, a bicycle (at the time of writing the first edition, eBay.co.uk was experimenting with a local listings section, but it looked unlikely to provide a successful alternative to small ads in the local newspaper). The 'Items located in United Kingdom' section could be helpful in saving on postage. The number of results per page you choose depends on the speed of your connection – go for 25 if it's slow, 100 if it's fast or you want to make a pot of tea while you wait.

There are many reasons why US sellers won't sell abroad. They range from fear of fraud to thinking that there are enough buyers in the US without having to bother with the extra hassle of posting abroad. The postal arrangements for mailing some items abroad can be more complicated in the US than they are here and there can be copyright restrictions, too. That said, many US sellers are happy to deal with customers almost anywhere, and I've only been ripped off once.

TIP

If you do a worldwide search and see something you really want advertised as 'US buyers only', send the seller an email via the 'Ask seller a question' button on the item description page, politely asking them to consider selling it to you (with, of course, an additional post & packing cost). If you've got decent feedback, this approach often works. Sometimes, after all, the seller has put 'US only' simply because it's the default position on the listings page.

A useful tip, if you're following auctions that attract a specialised kind of buyer, is to check out the other bidders. I've known of people who've buddied up with other eBayers to take it in turn to bid on items. This may not seem very 'fair' but it's perfectly legitimate, and not dissimilar to the rings which you get in offline auctions. I know of others who won't get involved in auctions when a particular buyer is involved because they know from past experience that he has very deep pockets.

The other thing you can do, if you notice a bidder frequently bidding in the same auctions as you, is to do a search on what items that bidder is currently bidding on (use the basic search then click on the 'items by bidder' tag on the left which will take you to the box shown opposite). You may discover things you want that you didn't know were currently being auctioned . . .

Fig 18.   Finding out what items another bidder is bidding on

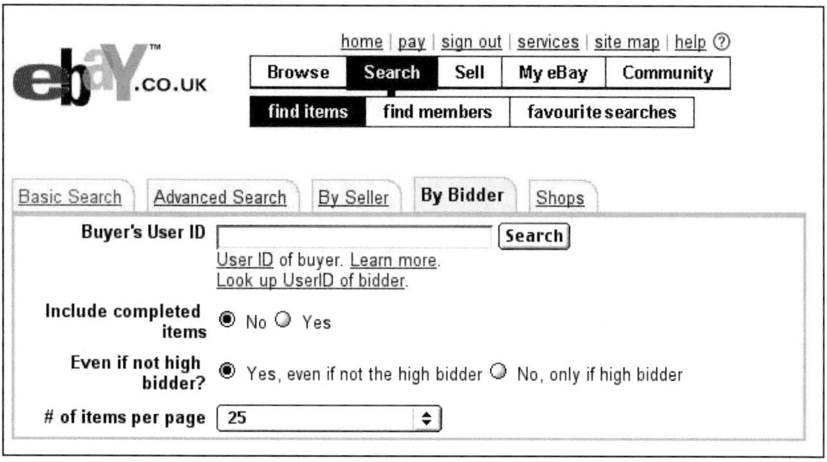

eBay is always changing . . .

A book like this will only scratch the surface of some specialist topics. Not only that, but eBay updates itself all the time, changing the way things work, testing things for a while then dropping them, and so on. For instance, while researching this book on a university PC a little while ago, I got a completely different eBay.co.uk screen to the one I usually get. At the bottom of the screen was a question: 'Why does this page look different?' with the answer that eBay was testing out new page designs for non-registered visitors. It thought I was a non-registered member because I was using a different PC to usual, and it could not find a cookie on the university machine.

There are information pages all over eBay (start at the site map) to explain their various innovations.

Using eBay forums

eBay also has what it calls 'forums', where eBay users talk to each other, sharing tips, news and moans. To find them, look at the 'Community' section of the site map.

Many of these forums are dominated by newbies (i.e. new users), but that's OK – you're a newbie too and are unlikely to get flamed (sent a bunch of insulting messages) if you ask a stupid question. Some of these forums are invaluable – 'technical and HTML issues' being the prime example. Others, like the one on postage and packing, may well be a comfort in your early eBay days. Personally, I never used them until I started researching this book, but I've found that some boards can be very helpful (and eBay employees often provide a kind of online help service by answering

> "Some forums are invaluable – 'technical and HTML issues' being the prime example."

posts). There is also an announcements board that is useful for keeping up to date with the latest developments.

Internet newsgroups

While I don't frequent the official eBay community boards, every day I spend a few minutes using the usenet newsgroup alt.marketing.online.ebay. I don't read every message, as this group averages at least three hundred posts a day, but I follow the threads that look interesting. Be warned though, this is a usenet newsgroup. Never put your email address online or you'll get far more spam than you already do. If you want personal replies, use a disguised email address that's easy to unpick like David@mypants.server.com with 'to reply, remove my pants' in the body of the message.

The usenet newsgroup, alt.marketing.online.ebay, is a fantastic resource for finding out what's happening on eBay worldwide and there are a lot of highly experienced eBay sellers who frequently post (and a fair few idiots, of course). If you ask a sensible question, you can expect a sensible reply. Ask a stupid one, and you can be made to feel like a fool. But most newsgroup readers don't post messages, they 'lurk', reading whatever interests them. It's definitely worth having a look, either by using a news reader programme (most service providers will give you the full range of newsgroups) or you can access it through Outlook Express or Google groups.

The UK group, uk.people.consumers.ebay, currently averages about a hundred posts a day. It's not as authoritative as alt.marketing.online.ebay but it's a friendly newsgroup that is more relevant to UK users. You may well find it a comfortable place to ask a (potentially) stupid question or let off steam about something that's gone wrong. The group has a very useful FAQ (answers to Frequently Asked Questions) at:

* upce.org.uk/

Sniping

'Sniping' is where a bidder makes a last-minute bid in order to win an auction without giving another bidder enough time to outbid them. Some snipers use sniping software that automatically places the bid for them at the time they choose, but this software isn't 100% reliable. Sniping takes some of the fun out of manual bidding. Many eBayers dislike sniping, but it isn't unethical. Arguably, it benefits the seller by raising the price beyond the maximum that the non-sniper was willing to pay.

The crucial thing to remember about sniping is that, as a non-sniping bidder, you won't lose out if you bid your true maximum. If the final price goes above your maximum, you wouldn't have bid it anyway and the sniper has saved you getting involved in a bidding war in the last few minutes of the auction (most eBayers have stories to tell about getting caught up in a live bidding frenzy at the end of the auction and paying more than they should).

As a buyer, when should you snipe? Part of the reason for sniping is to avoid being outbid by people who aren't sure of the item's maximum value and are also undecided about their own maximum bid. Sniping avoids giving these bidders the information they need (what another bidder is willing to pay) to make the right size winning bid. Snipers don't engage in live bidding wars, but their last-minute bids often increase final auction prices by large amounts, whether they win or lose.

Sellers gain from sniping, but some sellers feel it is against the 'spirit of eBay' and have been known to block bidders who use automatic sniping software or even leave negative feedback for them (this is not, as far as I can tell, a significant risk). I think the main point here is worth reiterating: if a non-sniper puts in their proxy bid for the maximum amount they're willing to pay, it doesn't matter if a higher bid is placed with nine days or nine seconds of the auction remaining – the result will be the same. Sniping takes advantage of people who foolishly bid less than they have in mind. These bidders expect to be able to manually counter anybody who outbids them. The prevalence of sniping discourages this behaviour and therefore encourages higher proxy bids, often increasing sellers' profits.

Automated tools?

One can argue that automated sniping is the way to go and I now use a couple of snipe sites to bid on most auctions. (Why two? Because both have periods when they don't work properly, which is one reason why I'm not endorsing a particular sniping site here.) You can schedule an automated snipe a day or several days in advance. If the software you use doesn't malfunction, this is the same as bidding your maximum but gives you an edge – you won't be tempting somebody to outbid you and raise their maximum. It also means that you can forget about the auction until you get the email telling you whether you've won or not. The sniping site that I use most also emails you if the current price on an auction exceeds the maximum bid in the snipe you've scheduled. Sniping makes bidding more efficient and it's a dog eat dog world (add your own cliché about the merciless nature of capitalism here). Whether you choose to do this is down to how you choose to behave on eBay – how serious you want to be and what spirit you approach auctions in. If you want to find a sniping site, do a Google search on 'eBay UK sniping software', you'll get plenty of hits. Take your pick. If you do use a sniping site, there are security issues. You have to give them your eBay password. This is another reason to change your password frequently and use a different one for Paypal. Where passwords are concerned, exercise caution at all times (more on this later).

How to pay

When I started selling on eBay, I used to specify that I took sterling cheques or well-concealed cash (at sender's risk). These days, as the illustration opposite shows, paying for goods is a lot more straightforward. If you look at the bottom of any eBay auction, you'll see the forms of payment that the seller accepts. Sellers who are commercial stores often take credit cards. Many private sellers take credit card payments through PayPal (before PayPal existed I used to get several spam messages a day, offering me the facility to take credit cards). In the UK, if PayPal sellers take credit cards, they used to be entitled to ask an extra fee to cover the costs PayPal charges in order to allow credit cards (see the section 'To PayPal or not to PayPal' on page 121). This is no longer the case (although some sellers try it on – if this happens to you as a buyer, politely point out that eBay does not allow you to pay surcharges) and eBay's new surcharging rules are set out in appendix 4 on pages 171-173.

Fig 19. Message to winning bidder

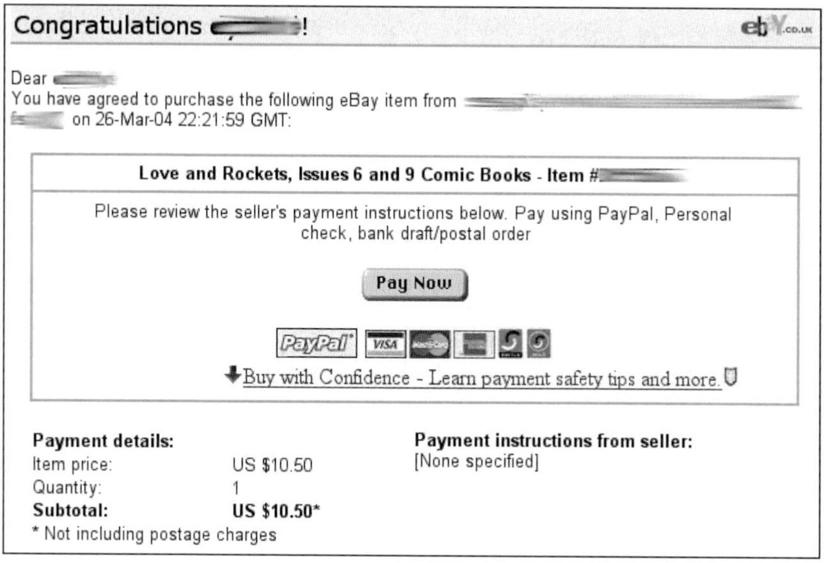

Congratulations ▢▢▢!   eb Y.co.uk

Dear ▢▢▢
You have agreed to purchase the following eBay item from ▢▢▢
▢▢▢ on 26-Mar-04 22:21:59 GMT:

Love and Rockets, Issues 6 and 9 Comic Books - Item #▢▢▢

Please review the seller's payment instructions below. Pay using PayPal, Personal check, bank draft/postal order

Pay Now

PayPal VISA ▢▢ ▢ ▢ ▢
♦ Buy with Confidence - Learn payment safety tips and more. ∪

Payment details: **Payment instructions from seller:**
Item price: US $10.50   [None specified]
Quantity: 1
Subtotal: **US $10.50***
* Not including postage charges

I still accept well-concealed cash but, since the advent of PayPal, few sellers offer this as an option. Dollars would reach me for a purchase then return to the US for one of my purchases. I have eighteen greenbacks in my spare wallet as I type, saved just in case I need to pay for a US item in cash. They've been there for more than two years. In the UK, cheques and postal orders are fine (though some sellers will delay sending goods until your cheque has cleared). But, as a buyer, if the seller accepts it, you might as well use PayPal.

PayPal

PayPal is a combination of an online bank and credit card company. It started up as a separate company but has since been bought by eBay. There are other online payment systems, but PayPal dominates to a massive extent. It's easy to register and, once you're on PayPal, instant payments are a piece of cake. Just one caveat: if you're mainly going to be a buyer, it's best to pay by credit card, rather than by keeping money in your PayPal account. This is because the protection against fraud on credit cards is better than the protection offered by eBay. If somebody takes your money and doesn't deliver the goods, you can do a 'chargeback' with your credit card company, which will force PayPal to reimburse you (though, be warned, if PayPal isn't happy with how you behaved, or you do it more than once, they're very likely to throw you off the system). If you've effectively used cash (your PayPal balance) then you're not on your own, but on a lowish price item, you might as well be. eBay won't even look at fraud complaints of less than twenty dollars.

PayPal is convenient, but I still use cash or cheques from time to time. A final warning – whether you use PayPal or not, you will get endless scam emails pretending to be from PayPal or eBay (see section 10). These will try to get you to visit their site (disguised to look like an official eBay or PayPal site) and reveal your log in details (password, User ID etc) so that they can steal money from your PayPal account or, more likely, use your account to do some buying of their own. You can report these emails by forwarding them to spoof@paypal.co.uk.

Feedback

Feedback is the bedrock of eBay, the foundation of the mutual trust that makes the eBay community work. The system is simple. After every transaction, each participant leaves feedback for the other: positive, negative or neutral. This feedback should be accompanied by a comment, up to eighty characters long.

Fig 20. Information about a seller's feedback

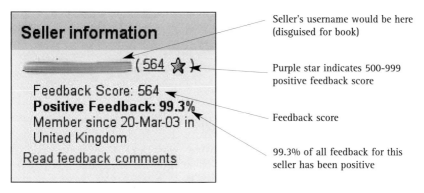

Seller's username would be here (disguised for book)

Purple star indicates 500-999 positive feedback score

Feedback score

99.3% of all feedback for this seller has been positive

When you bid on, or sell an item, your **feedback score** appears next to your User ID, as in the illustration above. The first figure is the number of transactions from unique users you have positive feedback on. (Transactions where no feedback was left don't count. Nor does feedback from repeat buyers and sellers, though these are shown in the detailed breakdown on your feedback page.) A negative figure means that your negative feedback is greater than your positive feedback. You don't see many of these!

The number of positive feedback points is less important than the number that appears beneath it – your percentage of positive feedbacks. If a seller has less than 98% feedback, you should think very seriously before bidding. Neutral feedback does not figure in these percentages but can still be read on the detailed feedback page.

Read the 'Check feedback before bidding' section in 'Buying on eBay' on page 33 if you haven't already. Sellers should note that, when you click on the buyer's feedback score you will also see the number of 'bid retractions' the buyer has made in the last six months. Bid retractions don't result in feedback, but could be a sign of shill bidding, so more than one retraction raises serious doubts.

Build feedback by buying

Unless you're really anxious to start selling straight away, it's best to build up some positive feedback by buying a few items first. Even if you intend to be mainly a seller, it's useful to get the feeling of how eBay works from a buyer's point of view, and you may pick up some useful tips, particularly if you buy the sort of item that you intend to sell. Note that buying multiple items from the same seller will not build your feedback score by more than one (although it counts in your percentages).

How to leave feedback

If you have a 'My eBay' page, click on the 'Feedback' link, as below:

This will take you to this link:

Fig 21. Feedback link page

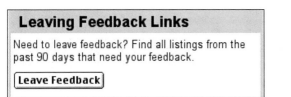

Click on 'Leave Feedback' and you will be taken to a page that shows all the feedback you need to leave.

Fig 22. Finding out what feedback you need to leave

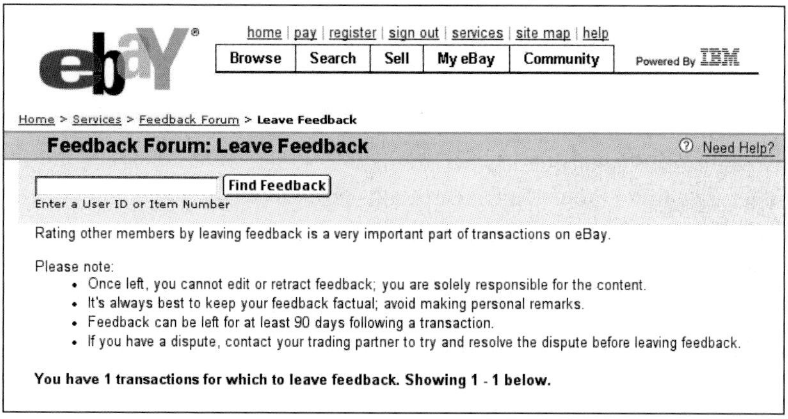

You don't have to leave feedback until you're ready. When you do, highlight the circle for positive, negative or neutral, then leave a comment up to eighty characters long.

Fig 23. Leaving feedback

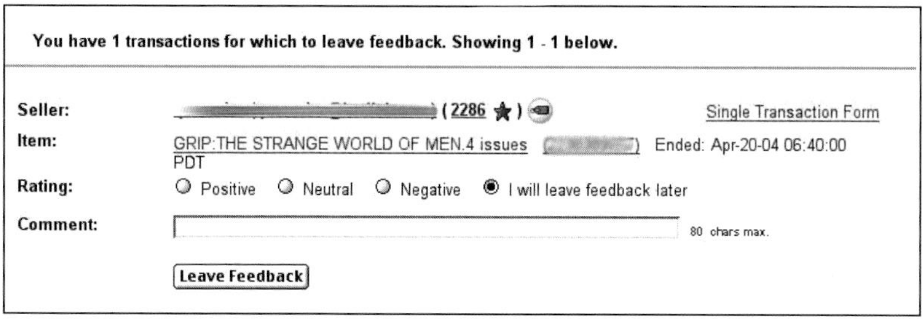

If you're not using 'My eBay' yet, you can go to the original item page (there will be links to this on your email from eBay informing you of your successful bid) and follow the link to leave feedback.

Always leave feedback

If you win an auction and get the goods delivered as described, you should leave positive feedback, whether or not the seller has already left feedback for you. Some sellers don't leave feedback until after the buyer has. There are constant discussions amongst sellers as to whether this is fair or not. Personally, I always leave feedback as soon as someone has paid.

The only exception is when they pay by personal cheque. Then, if the buyer has a 100 percent feedback record, I post the item straight away, and send a note saying that I will leave positive feedback when their cheque has cleared. But maybe I'm too soft. Many sellers are more cautious, waiting for cheques to clear before sending goods and only leaving feedback after buyers have. This gives them the opportunity to leave negative retaliatory feedback should the buyer negative them. But nearly all negatives are avoidable if the aggrieved party communicates with the other party or, if that doesn't work, follows eBay's dispute resolution procedures (see 'Frauds, scams, deadbeat bidders and vigilantes' on page 137).

Only leave negative feedback as a last resort

Some sellers never leave feedback. Many wait to leave feedback because of an understandable fear: if the seller hasn't left feedback for the buyer, the buyer is much less likely to negative them, as they risk being negatived themselves. This might seem unfair, but the risk of negative feedback from either side helps to keep everybody honest.

Most negative feedback is left for and by newbies, who don't fully understand how the system works. That's why, when you leave negative or neutral feedback, eBay will give you a warning that you are responsible for your words and give you an opportunity not to go ahead. In 2005, eBay added a compulsory tutorial for those with less than ten positives leaving a negative. This might sound draconian, but don't underestimate how important negative feedback is. A big seller can take a handful of unjustified negatives, as it won't affect their positives percentage too much. A small seller can be badly hit by even one negative. I don't know of any instances where people have been sued for libel over unjustifiable negative feedback, but it's bound to happen one of these days.

In my several years of trading on eBay, I have only left negative feedback once and neutral feedback once. In the first instance, I came up against an unabashed thief, who is still trading, and is discussed anonymously in the 'Fraud' section on pages 147-148. In the other, I neutralled a new seller who didn't reply to my complaint. I politely pointed out that he'd sent me a comic which wasn't as described. I had emailed him using the 'Ask the seller a question' link on the item description page to check that the comic in question was a first edition, not a much later reprint. He'd replied that it was, but on arrival it clearly wasn't. To compound the problem, he'd packaged the comic in a good, but inappropriate, wrapper, so that it arrived in a crushed state. I sent a polite email, pointing this out, and gave him three days to reply, then left a neutral. It was a cheap item and a negative seemed over the top. I might have ignored the transaction if he'd apologised or offered a refund, but he didn't. Here's the dialogue, which I just called up using a tool we'll discuss a little later on:

Fig 24. Example of negative feedback and seller's reply

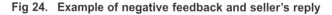

Comment	Left For	Date / Time	Item #
⊙ Comic poorly packaged and a reprint not original. No response to complaint. **Reply by** ▬▬▬: no other complaints, packaging left fine, no time to respond to complaint	Seller ▬▬▬ (201 ☆)	Sep-02-03 05:54 / Sep-02-03 09:33	▬▬▬

This seller had only a handful of positives at the time and, I found from checking his feedback, it was his first time as a seller. You can see from the feedback number above ('201'), that he has gone on to trade successfully. In his response to my feedback, he doesn't respond to the most important complaint (the comic being a reprint) but his reply looks convincing enough not to put off other buyers, especially when he has no negative feedback. Neutrals don't figure in eBay's feedback calculations. This

> "The risk of negative feedback from either side helps to keep everybody honest."

guy now has 100 percent feedback, with no other neutrals. I'll bet he never misdescribed an item again. I felt awkward about leaving a newbie a neutral, but it gave him a useful kick up the backside, and that's how feedback's supposed to work.

I should add that I felt more empowered to leave a neutral because the seller above had already left positive feedback for me. **You only get to leave feedback once, and may only respond to feedback once** (getting feedback removed is so difficult that it's hardly worth doing, as we'll discuss later).

Had my seller not already left feedback, would I have left neutral feedback? Probably, but some users would wait until the last moment (ninety days after the auction ends is when the link to 'Leave feedback' expires) so that he wouldn't have time to leave a retaliatory negative. Note that you can always respond to bad feedback left about you (and should do, otherwise it looks like you accept that you were fully at fault).

If you want to know how likely it is that someone will negative or neutral you, go to the user's feedback profile (or use the method described in the box below) and click on the 'Feedback about others' link to see if they often leave feedback and whether they respond tit-for-tat to negatives.

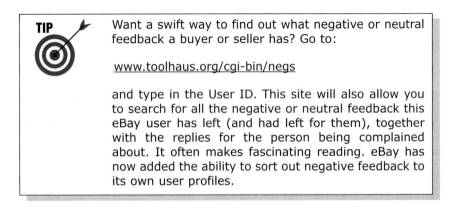

TIP Want a swift way to find out what negative or neutral feedback a buyer or seller has? Go to:

www.toolhaus.org/cgi-bin/negs

and type in the User ID. This site will also allow you to search for all the negative or neutral feedback this eBay user has left (and had left for them), together with the replies for the person being complained about. It often makes fascinating reading. eBay has now added the ability to sort out negative feedback to its own user profiles.

Feedback exhortation

Not everybody leaves feedback. It's a voluntary system and you can't force people to use it. Pressuring eBayers to leave feedback can often have negative results. For instance, a book seller sent me a book with a nice handwritten note saying that he would happily leave feedback for me after I'd left it for him. I ignored it, because the book wasn't quite in the description described (he had failed to note that it had some shotgun pellet stuck in the binding – I'd be interested to know the story behind that flaw). The book wasn't valuable enough for me to think the flaw worth complaining about, but I certainly wasn't going to leave positive feedback. The creepy, solicitous note made me far more likely to negative him. In situations where you're not happy, but the problems aren't big enough to waste time by making them into an issue, leaving no feedback is the right way to behave.

If you're dealing with individuals, often small traders like yourself, it's worth mentioning that you've left feedback. This is where leaving feedback as soon as you've got payment can help you build your feedback profile. A note saying "Payment received, item in post, positive feedback left – be grateful if you'd do the same if you're happy when it arrives, but any problems, let me know" is, in a manner of speaking, feedback exhortation, but almost always works.

A warning. There are sellers who run auctions selling small items (often vouchers for money off a bigger item or free downloads) for piffling amounts in order to build up their positive feedback. Many of these go on to run fraudulent or, at the very least, highly dubious auctions. Don't go near them.

If sellers say you haven't got enough feedback

As a buyer, after your first few positive feedbacks are left, your feedback will be of less importance to you than it is when you're a seller. You don't need to pay it much attention. However, sellers do have the power to block bidders or remove them from an auction. This should only be done if the bidder has violated the terms of the auction, say by bidding from a country the seller has said they won't accept bids from, or having a negative or low feedback rating when the seller has said such bidders are excluded (a warning you see much less often than you used to). If you see an auction where buyers who merely have low feedback are excluded and you really want to bid, it's worth emailing the seller a question. Point out that you're a newbie but understand the auction system and have the means to pay promptly. In most circumstances, the seller will relent and let you bid.

Sellers rely on their feedback record

As a seller, feedback remains crucial throughout your eBay selling career. High volume sellers can expect to get a few negatives for all sorts of reasons. If their overall positive percentage remains near the 100 mark, this shouldn't matter too much. But a canny buyer can always search to find the negative feedback and judge for themselves. For instance, a magazine subscription auction site has 'Buy It Now' prices that look too good to be true, so I look at the seller information:

Fig 25. Example of seller information

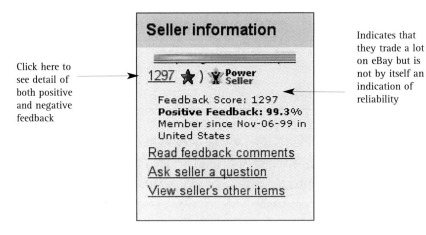

That they're a 'Power Seller' means they do a lot of business through eBay but doesn't guarantee that they're any more reliable than a seller with much smaller turnover.

A search through their negative feedback, by clicking on the '1297' in the box above, will tell me if there are any likely problems that aren't mentioned in their ad (which warns that their subscriptions take a long time to start and are only available in the US). I find a dozen complaints – more neutrals than negatives – and the seller has replied to each one, with rational, convincing points (not always easy, when you only have eighty characters to play with). If I lived in the US and wanted a four year subscription to Rolling Stone for ten dollars, I'd certainly give her my money.

Private feedback

It is possible to make your feedback private so that nobody but you can read it. However, I'd be very suspicious of anybody whose feedback is made private. The most likely reason is that they've had a lot of recent negatives but their positive percentage (which can't be kept secret) is still high enough not to put off bidders. If a seller has private feedback, I'd think twice before bidding and then think again.

Feedback withdrawal

eBay doesn't make it easy to get feedback withdrawn. In the past, they have charged offputting fees and made the process complicated. In 2004, they introduced 'mutual feedback withdrawal', a system that allows buyer and seller to agree when feedback was left in error and withdraw it. The comments (including any follow-up) will remain viewable, but the feedback will not affect either party's feedback score. Mutual feedback withdrawal must take place within thirty days of feedback being left or within ninety days of the transaction, whichever is longer. There is no fee.

Mutual feedback withdrawal requires cooperation between the two disagreeing parties, which is in keeping with eBay's philosophy, but does mean that it could be tricky to negotiate if dealing with an inexperienced new user. One final thing to note on this is that, if one of the parties in the transaction has yet to leave feedback, they forfeit their right to do so after the mutual withdrawal. Since the page is hard to track down, here's a URL for the information page that includes a link to the mutual withdrawal form:

- pages.ebay.co.uk/help/account/withdraw-feedback.html

Feedback removal

eBay will remove feedback only under fairly extreme circumstances. The most effective one is a court order (remember, you are liable for what you say in feedback and can be sued for libel). The legal definition of libel is that you write something about another living person which is likely to damage that person's reputation and *which is untrue.* If what you write is true, then it is not libelous, so eBayers who feel strongly that another person has done something wrong, and who think they could prove it in court, can make that view public in feedback in the knowledge that the law is on their side. However, the burden of proof in a libel action is on the person being sued. If someone sues you for libel because of what you have written about them on eBay, it is up to you to prove that it was true and therefore not libelous. That may not be easy to do.

Other reasons eBay might agree to remove feedback include profane or racist language, feedback including confidential contact information, feedback containing links, references to an eBay or other official investigation, feedback by a member who has either been NARU'd or who should have been NARU'd at the time they left the feedback (i.e. for providing false contact information).

Note the following eBay policy:

"Negative feedback intended for another member will be considered for removal only in situations where the member responsible for the mistaken posting has already placed the same feedback for the correct member."

This rules out the most convincing excuse for leaving the wrong feedback ('oops, wrong guy!') if you suddenly realise that you've said something ill-advised. This policy reinforces the point that you are responsible for the feedback you leave, so ought to think very carefully about what you write before leaving a neutral or negative.

Finally, although feedback is important, remember that it's voluntary. Between a quarter and a third of users don't leave it, so don't break into a sweat about the ones who don't leave any for you, even when you've left it for them.

NOTE! The acronym 'NARU' means 'no longer a registered user' or, less prosaically, 'thrown off eBay'. eBay operates a 'three strikes and you're out' policy for users who break the rules, although serious infractions can result in being instantly NARU'd and some users get away with having many complaints spread over a long period. The weakness of the system is that it's fairly easy to re-register under a new User ID with changed contact info, but, in such instances, users lose all of their feedback.

Dare to sell

• •

A profitable hobby

I treat eBay as a low-cost hobby. For the most part, I fund new purchases by selling old ones. I'm not alone. The sellers of that 'Lost In Translation' DVD had probably bought the DVD as soon as it was released in the US, watched it once, then sold it on, making only a tiny loss. They'd have seen the movie for far less than it would have cost to rent it (if it was available) or see it at the cinema (if

> "You don't have to be a cheapskate to do well on eBay but it helps."

it was showing near them). They saved on storage space, too. The only extra cost is in time – a few minutes to post the auction and a couple more to sort out payment details and post the DVD.

Most writers I know are tight with money: we've often had to get by without any. You don't have to be a cheapskate to do well on eBay, but it helps. It's a game, trying to get stuff for the lowest price when you could easily afford the full cost. Calculate the cost of time spent browsing before bidding at anything approaching the national minimum wage and it will probably turn out the item isn't even that cheap. But browsing is fun. And so is selling. In this section, I go through the basics of selling.

British reserve

You've registered as a seller and you've chosen to sell your – let's say it's a toilet seat – in an online auction. (The 'Buy It Now' option is covered on page 81.)

First question: should you use a reserve? If you do, you can set a starting bid well below the amount you are willing to accept for the toilet seat (but you will pay a listing fee based on the size of the reserve, plus an extra fee – see page 163 for details of fees). This low price may attract more bidders to get involved. If a bidder's maximum bid is high enough, the reserve will automatically be met, even if there are no other bidders. If the bidding does not go as high as your reserve, you won't have to sell the item.

Note that many buyers are put off by reserves. They see a note beneath the starting bid saying 'reserve not met' which is in itself offputting. Buyers have no way of knowing what the reserve is unless they make a high enough bid or they write and ask you. If this happens, you should tell them. **Research tends to show that items with higher starting bids and no reserve do better than the other way round.**

Setting the starting bid

Before you put an item up for sale, research other sellers who trade in the same item. Find out what they put as a starting bid and how much their items tend to go for. If you're putting up a high-value item, consider using a reserve, rather than an offputtingly-high starting bid. That said, I never use reserves. Instead, I set a starting bid that is the lowest amount I will happily accept for an item – say £1.99 for a single or £4.99 for a CD that isn't particularly rare.

You can get around most listing fees by using eBay's occasional free or cheap listing days (these have their risks – see 'There's no such thing as a free listings day' on page 113). If you start the bidding at 1p, you are likely to get more bidders, though most will drop out when the toilet seat reaches a realistic price. One of my favourite online stores, Marie's CDs and Online Auctions (formerly 'Jay and Marie's one cent CDs') in San Diego uses this tactic. They are the biggest dealer on eBay, with over 222,222 positive feedback comments from unique users.

How do you know what an item is worth?

An item is worth what somebody is willing to pay for it. The best way to work out the value of something you plan to sell is by tracking auctions for similar items for a few days or weeks. See how similar the item is to yours in regard to age, condition and any other relevant criteria. Of course, this takes time, but if it's the kind of item that you might plan to sell frequently, it really helps to know the market. And there's a shortcut. If you use eBay's 'Advanced Search', you can search by 'Completed items only' which will take you to a list of auctions that have actually closed out with a sale (i.e. real, achieved prices), leaving out auctions which are either still in progress or that never resulted in a sale. (eBay now includes a link to completed items search on some versions of the basic search page.)

Fig 26. Advanced search page

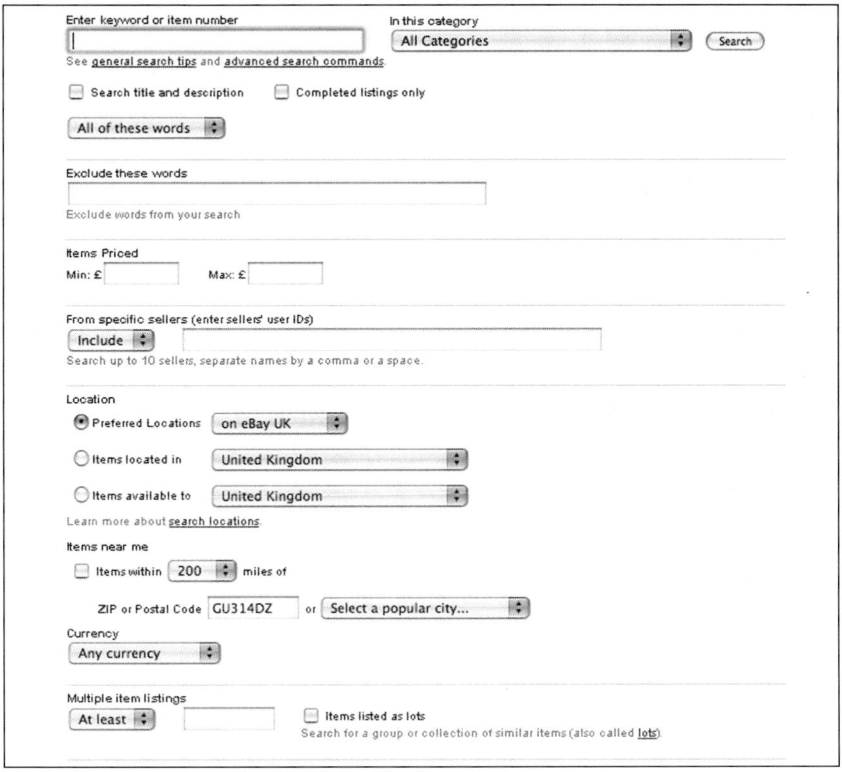

Enter keyword or item number | In this category

| | | All Categories | | Search |

See general search tips and advanced search commands.

☐ Search title and description   ☐ Completed listings only

All of these words

Exclude these words

Exclude words from your search

Items Priced
Min: £   Max: £

From specific sellers (enter sellers' user IDs)
Include
Search up to 10 sellers, separate names by a comma or a space.

Location
◉ Preferred Locations   on eBay UK
○ Items located in   United Kingdom
○ Items available to   United Kingdom
Learn more about search locations.

Items near me
☐ Items within   200   miles of
ZIP or Postal Code GU314DZ   or Select a popular city...

Currency
Any currency

Multiple item listings
At least   ☐ Items listed as lots
Search for a group or collection of similar items (also called lots).

The best place to find out what something sells for on eBay is . . . eBay. In many collecting fields, it has become the main source of pricing information. But there are other ways. Use price guide books for many collectable items (a quick search on Amazon.co.uk, typing in the name of the kind of item you're selling plus 'price guide', should tell you if one exists e.g. 'Hornby trains price guide'). Some price guides have an online version.

For less collectable stuff, *Exchange & Mart*, ads in the back of papers, and even car boot sales will tell you what the rock bottom price is for the item you're selling. You may want to make the car boot price your starting bid. It's rare that you won't do better on eBay. There are people who make a living by buying at car boot sales and reselling on eBay, but you have to get up early at the weekend to become one of them.

Grade accurately

When selling an item, be sure to describe it as accurately as possible. Nothing annoys a buyer more than buying an item that is not in the condition described. It's best to always err on the side of caution. If you undergrade an item, and a buyer gives you feedback saying 'item in better condition than described', that's a great ad. The opposite (especially if accompanied by negative or neutral feedback) is really bad news, more so if you are a new seller.

> "There are people who make a living by buying at car boot sales and reselling on eBay but you have to get up early at the weekend to become one of them."

As for what grading system to use, this depends on the item. 'As new' will work for some things. 'A++' for others. But, for vinyl records, for instance, there are very specific grading criteria, and the same applies to many specialist collectables. A Google search using the words 'record collector grading' will throw up these criteria and a similar search will work for some other collectables.

If you plan to sell lots of a particular kind of collectable item, it might be worth investing in a price guide for the collectable: it will include detailed grading advice (search Amazon and note that second-hand, out-of-date price guides are rarely worth owning). Even if you're selling an item that's as common as mud, avoid bland, meaningless descriptions of the 'really nice' or 'good for its age' kind. Be as specific as you can be about flaws. Many people don't mind getting things that are slightly damaged because they either can't afford a perfect version or prefer getting a bargain.

As a rough guide, where collectables are concerned, condition descriptions range from 'Mint' (e.g. unread or unplayed, perhaps still in shrink wrap), through 'Excellent', 'Very Good', 'Good', 'Fair' and 'Poor' to 'Bad' (unplayable or unreadable, only a lunatic would buy it). It's rarely worth selling something in less than fair condition and, even then, it might be worth only a tenth of the mint price.

Good descriptions will give the buyer confidence. With some auctions, using a scanned image can also help a sale (if you do this to describe condition, make it clear that the image is of the actual item, as many sellers use stock images to illustrate their auctions). The use of images is discussed more fully in Section 9.

1, 3, 5, 7 or 10 days?

When you first list an item for sale, eBay asks you to decide how long your auction will last. 1, 3, 5, 7 and 10 days are the basic auction deadline choices, although if you use 'Buy It Now' they can become irrelevant (see 'Auction or Buy It Now?' on page 107). Unless, for some reason, you're in a real hurry for the money, the longer periods are more likely to produce the best price, for the simple reason that more people are likely to see the auction. 1-day auctions are only of use for things that, for whatever reason, have a very short shelf life, like tickets for a sports event. It can take several hours for new items to show up in eBay's search engines, so much of the day is wasted.

When is it best to end an auction?

A more important calculation than the length of auction can be the start and end time. eBay offers you a facility to start your auction at a fixed time (it currently charges 12p a listing for this). You can also set auctions to begin days in advance. If you decide that you want a 10-day auction and that the best time for it to end is at 7pm on a Sunday, but you don't want to be at your computer at that time ten days before, then 12p may well be worth it. For some items, getting in two Sundays, and ending the auction at midnight on a Sunday, when the buyer is trying to make that weekend feeling last, might be perfect timing. Ending a UK auction at midnight also makes it possible for US bidders in both the main time zones to be near their computer at the auction end. But nobody wants to be inputting auctions at midnight on a Thursday. 12p is a small price to pay to save on inconvenience and get a shot at someone paying silly money for your item.

If your item has strong international appeal, do **bear time differences in mind**. Many people argue that early to mid-evening midweek times are the best times for auctions to end after buyers get home from work. But it depends on what you're selling and where you're selling to. Some buyers only use eBay at work. Others are restricted to home. When you've been selling for a while, you should be able to get a sense of what time of day your bidders make their first bids (rather than their later bids that rise by automatic proxy) and set your end times accordingly. Also bear in mind that automatic sniping tools make end times irrelevant for some buyers.

There are times when it's worth setting a 3-day auction deadline, for instance, for tickets where the event takes place in the next week or two. Another example would be something that is rare, but soon won't be as rare. In the UK, record companies often sell limited edition vinyl singles that go for stratospheric prices in the first week of release. But if a lot of people buy them to sell on, the eBay price soon stabilises as US or

> "On eBay, the default position is for the auctions ending soonest to be listed first."

Japanese buyers quickly realise that there's a large supply and they don't have to pay so much. If you were selling these items, you wouldn't want to set a long auction period, because their value reduces as time passes. New film releases (or promotional paraphernalia) and stuff that buyers want to get quickly would be another item where a quick sale would be advisable.

Bear in mind too that, in a search on eBay, the default position is for the auctions ending soonest to be listed first. If you're selling a common item, there's less reason to have a long auction, as many buyers won't bother going through page after page of entries on their search, they'll only look at the ones ending soon.

There are other decisions to be made before getting ready to start your sale. If your item definitely requires an original image, read the section on using photos first. If it requires specialist postage and packing, work out the price in advance of your listing – postage considerations may well help you decide what countries you're willing to sell to. Generally, though, you should only charge a little more than it actually costs to post and pack the item, rounding up the price to the nearest 50p or £1 to cover the cost of your time.

Start selling

Press the 'sell' button and you'll probably be asked to sign in. You'll be taken to this page:

Fig 27. Listing an item for sale

We're looking at auctions rather than the fixed price 'Buy It Now' option, so click 'Continue'. Next, you have to choose a category for your auction (you can short-step this process if you know the category number that you wish to sell under). This will help you define where your item belongs. Work your way through the boxes illustrated overleaf, or search by putting keywords in the box on the right and clicking 'Find'.

Fig 28. Choosing categories for your item

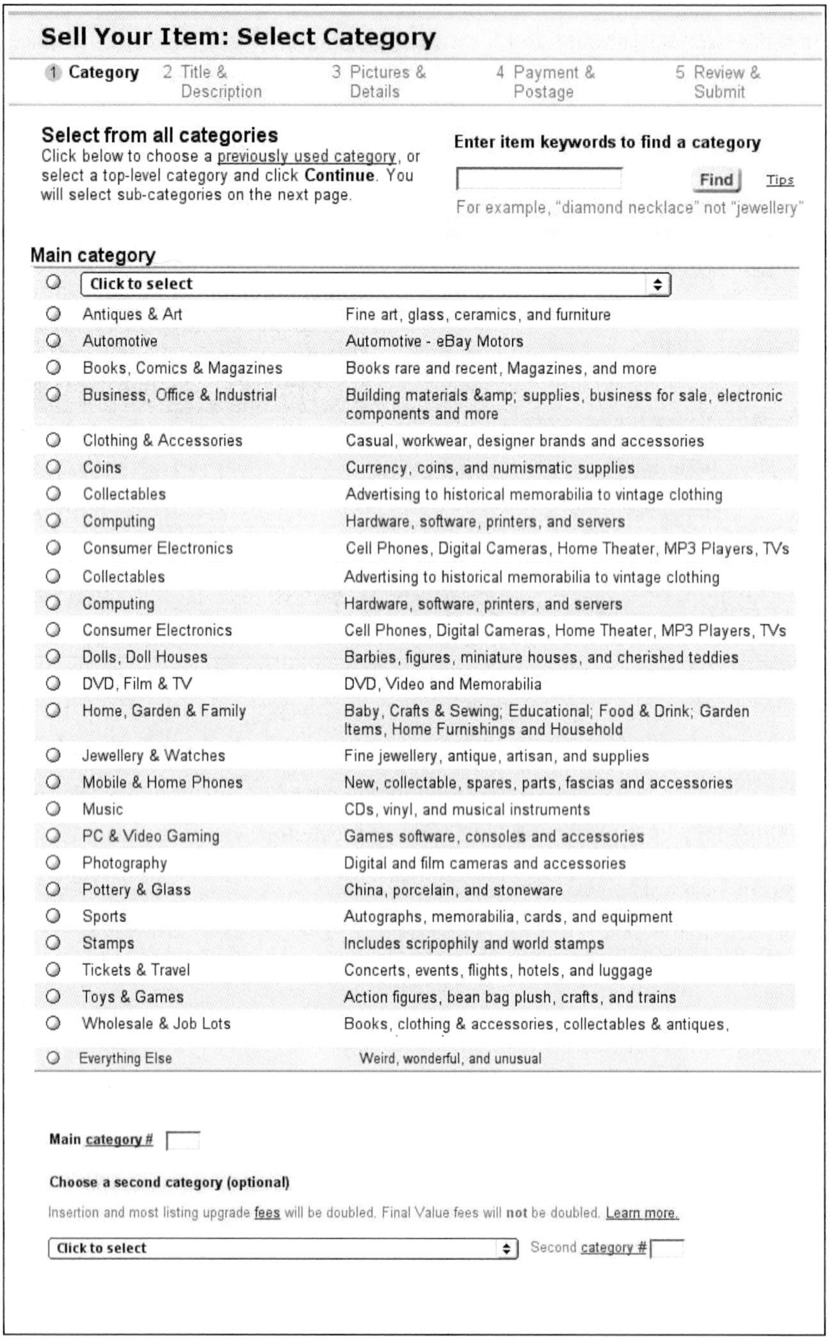

Sell Your Item: Select Category

① Category	2 Title & Description	3 Pictures & Details	4 Payment & Postage	5 Review & Submit

Select from all categories
Click below to choose a previously used category, or select a top-level category and click **Continue**. You will select sub-categories on the next page.

Enter item keywords to find a category

[ ] Find   Tips

For example, "diamond necklace" not "jewellery"

Main category

○	Click to select	♦
○	Antiques & Art	Fine art, glass, ceramics, and furniture
○	Automotive	Automotive - eBay Motors
○	Books, Comics & Magazines	Books rare and recent, Magazines, and more
○	Business, Office & Industrial	Building materials & supplies, business for sale, electronic components and more
○	Clothing & Accessories	Casual, workwear, designer brands and accessories
○	Coins	Currency, coins, and numismatic supplies
○	Collectables	Advertising to historical memorabilia to vintage clothing
○	Computing	Hardware, software, printers, and servers
○	Consumer Electronics	Cell Phones, Digital Cameras, Home Theater, MP3 Players, TVs
○	Collectables	Advertising to historical memorabilia to vintage clothing
○	Computing	Hardware, software, printers, and servers
○	Consumer Electronics	Cell Phones, Digital Cameras, Home Theater, MP3 Players, TVs
○	Dolls, Doll Houses	Barbies, figures, miniature houses, and cherished teddies
○	DVD, Film & TV	DVD, Video and Memorabilia
○	Home, Garden & Family	Baby, Crafts & Sewing; Educational; Food & Drink; Garden Items, Home Furnishings and Household
○	Jewellery & Watches	Fine jewellery, antique, artisan, and supplies
○	Mobile & Home Phones	New, collectable, spares, parts, fascias and accessories
○	Music	CDs, vinyl, and musical instruments
○	PC & Video Gaming	Games software, consoles and accessories
○	Photography	Digital and film cameras and accessories
○	Pottery & Glass	China, porcelain, and stoneware
○	Sports	Autographs, memorabilia, cards, and equipment
○	Stamps	Includes scripophily and world stamps
○	Tickets & Travel	Concerts, events, flights, hotels, and luggage
○	Toys & Games	Action figures, bean bag plush, crafts, and trains
○	Wholesale & Job Lots	Books, clothing & accessories, collectables & antiques,
○	Everything Else	Weird, wonderful, and unusual

Main category # [ ]

Choose a second category (optional)

Insertion and most listing upgrade fees will be doubled. Final Value fees will **not** be doubled. Learn more.

Click to select ♦ Second category # [ ]

You can add a second category (for an additional fee, though sometimes this is waived), but don't break sweat choosing categories unless you're selling something so specialist that buyers can regularly browse everything on sale in that category. Far more important – probably most important of all – is the auction title.

Choose your auction title carefully

You only have fifty-five characters to play with and that includes spaces, so you want to make the most of them. Exclamation marks and other typographical devices to gain attention are a waste of time – more likely to put buyers off than to attract them. Before you choose a title, think carefully about what words somebody doing a search for this item might type into the eBay search box. These are called 'keywords'. Include any keywords that a bidder might put into a search (e.g. add 'rare' as well as 'out of print' and 'OOP' or whatever the relevant terms are for the item you're selling). Make your description as well written as you can, but don't go over the top, as this can also put buyers off. Better, for some items, is pasting in reviews or item specs that help to describe and sell the item you're offering. Try to be as detailed as the character length allows so that buyers can identify from the title alone what it is they're going to click to have a look at. Include brand names and what the item is, even if you're listed in a category with the same name (because most people don't search through categories).

Fig 29.   Choosing a title and subtitle

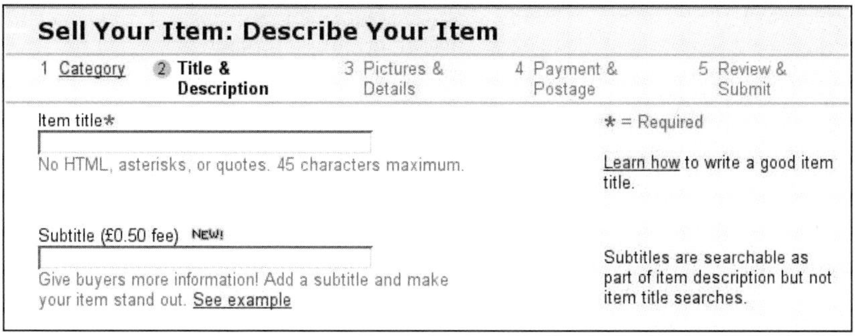

Sell Your Item: Describe Your Item

1 Category	② Title & Description	3 Pictures & Details	4 Payment & Postage	5 Review & Submit

Item title*

No HTML, asterisks, or quotes. 45 characters maximum.

* = Required

Learn how to write a good item title.

Subtitle (£0.50 fee) NEW!

Give buyers more information! Add a subtitle and make your item stand out. See example

Subtitles are searchable as part of item description but not item title searches.

If you give a general description, hoping that a buyer will click on to see precisely what the item is, you'll be losing an awful lot of potential buyers who can't be bothered to wait for your page to load on the off chance that it's going to be something they're interested in. You're not allowed to use email addresses or URLs in your title. Nor should you use words like "prohibited", "banned", "illegal" or "outlawed". These suggest you shouldn't be selling them on eBay. Obscenities are banned too, for obvious reasons.

Item description

Make this as detailed as possible, without going crazy. If it's a very common item, a simple description together with a clear statement of condition will suffice. For instance: '2005 book by David Belbin published by Harriman House. Unread, as new' might do as a description of the book you're holding, especially if you also provide a scan of the cover. To improve your selling chances, you might want to add a bit more detail about what the book contains. Many sellers of entertainment items like books even include brief extracts from rave reviews of the item being sold. This can't hurt. eBay offers prefilled information for cars, CDs and DVDs which can save you a bunch of time, but will also make your listing look like everyone else's. Make sure you include any individual points that might make the item seem more attractive.

Fig 30. Giving your item a description

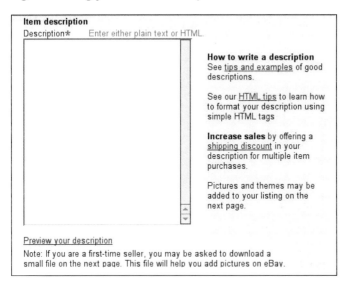

Occasionally things go wrong in the listing process (particularly if you have to leave your listings page and then return to it). Even if you have unmetered broadband access, it's worth writing your description offline and pasting it into the box, because if something does go wrong, you'll still have the text and won't have to go to the trouble of making it up and typing it out all over again.

Setting the starting bid on your item

A reminder: the 'starting bid' is the price you set when you list an item. It is also called the 'minimum bid' , 'opening bid' or 'opening price'. Buyers cannot bid lower than the minimum, and the first bid in an auction will always be at the minimum, even if the bidder's maximum is higher.

The lower you set the starting bid, the more bidders you're likely to get, and the cheaper your listing fee to eBay (see page 163). If you've done the research I recommend, you should have a fair idea of how popular the item you're selling is. If it's very common or, conversely, an item that's rarely sold on eBay, setting a starting bid at 1p may not be too clever. A penny may be all you get. Starting low is a calculated risk. The money you save on listing fees may justify taking the occasional bath. You have to find out what works for you. Generally, unless you set the starting bid way too high, it doesn't make a huge amount of difference.

'Buy It Now'

Whether or not you add a 'Buy It Now' option to your auction, and what BIN price you set, is another tricky decision. 'Buy It Now', remember, allows a buyer to snap up an item at the BIN price and to bring the auction to an immediate end. If you set the BIN price too low, you risk selling the item too cheaply. If you set it too high, it is likely to get BIN-stomped (see overleaf).

But even if no-one takes up the BIN offer, it can have an effect on an auction by indicating to browsers the sort of price you're willing to accept for the item and, possibly, the sort of price you're expecting (or hoping – not always the same thing) to get for it.

Typically, a seller who is running a business selling new items will set the starting bid at something like the wholesale price of an item and the BIN price at a reasonable retail price. For rarities or collectables, this calculation is much more difficult. The BIN price could be around the price that you expect the item to fetch at auction, or it could be significantly higher, in the hope of tempting a newbie with deep pockets.

The higher the BIN price, the more likely it is that somebody will make a preemptive bid to remove the price. This is called 'BIN-stomping'. **As soon as a bid of any size is made, the BIN option disappears** (unless you have also used a reserve that the bid does not meet). The purpose of BIN-stomping is that it prevents impulsive buyers from buying at the BIN price and thus interfering with the BIN-stomper's attempt to get the item for a much lower price at auction.

Note two things. Firstly, partly because of BIN-stomping, the size of your BIN price does not affect the listing fee. Secondly, so far we have only talked about adding a BIN option to an auction. It is also possible to list an item as 'BIN-only', (i.e. no auction) and this is discussed on pages 107-109.

Using pictures

eBay allows you one free picture with your listing so it makes sense to use one when you can. If you use a stock image (an image that is not of the specific item but is identical to it – like, say, the cover of a book) you should say so. In practice, few sellers do. If you have your own web space, you can link to an image that you have elsewhere online.

At the start, it's probably simplest to use eBay's picture hosting service. To do that, you need to know where the image is on your computer (I usually keep mine on the desktop) and click 'browse', then select the picture you want to use.

When you finish the page and click 'continue', a box will come up warning that it may take a few minutes for your image to load. However, unless you're using a huge image (which will be resized to make it more loadable) or are using a twentieth century modem, it's unlikely to take as long as a minute. This is covered more fully in the 'Using pictures and HTML' section on page 131.

Listing designer

You can add boldface (75p) or a coloured band (called 'highlight' - £1.50) to your listing. This might be worth doing if you're selling a fairly common, relatively expensive item that you want to stand out from the rest. eBay claims that items using boldface sell, on average, for 39% more than those without. It's worth considering.

eBay's 'listing designer' allows you to add background colour, pictures, and other improvements to your description:

Fig 31. Listing designer

You can choose a theme by selecting it in this drop-down box. The choices in the box below change according to the theme chosen

A preview of the theme will appear here

You can also choose a layout for your listing. This will place your descriptive text and pictures into a preformed layout. Choose the layout by clicking on your choice

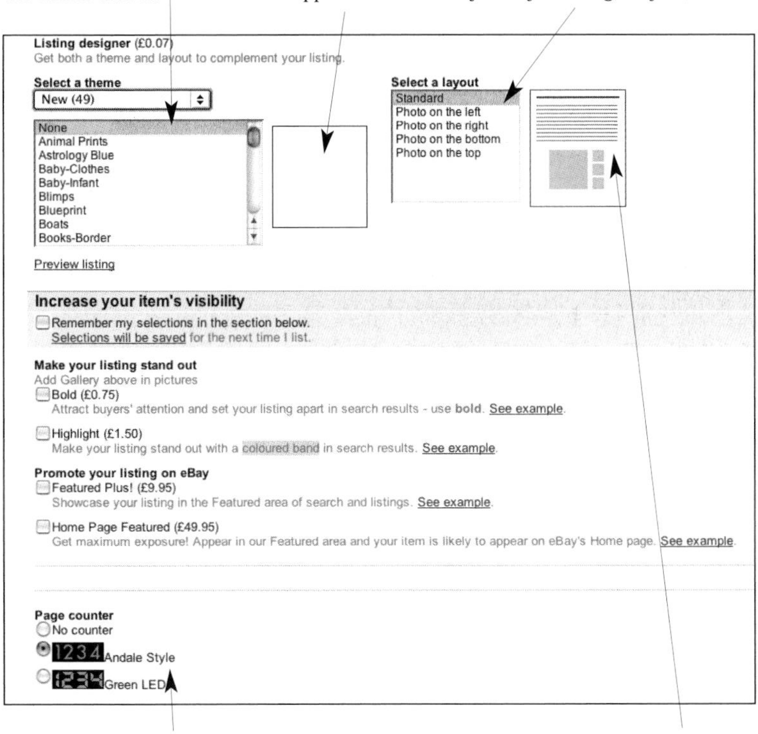

You can insert a page counter to see how often your auction has been viewed. There's no extra cost for this.

A preview of the layout will appear in this box

If you have HTML tags in your description, they will still work when you use Listing designer. I usually put a page counter on my auctions. This allows you to see how many times your page has been viewed, which is essential auction information, but a double-edged sword, because it allows bidders to know how popular an auction is, and judge their bid accordingly.

Where to sell to

The details form will also ask you to state where you are in the UK (or you can tick the box marked 'don't list regionally'). You will be asked to say where you'll sell to. The first time that you sell is particularly important because eBay will remember your preferences for every auction you set up in the future. (It always allows you to change them, though, and will remember your most recent auction.) There's a separate box where you should spell out your post and packing charges. Some sellers put this in the description box because newbies don't always know they have to look below for these details.

If you're willing to sell abroad, make sure you've worked out a price for the main zones. As a rule of thumb, Europe costs less to post to than the rest of the world, so it's often best to quote three price levels – UK, EC or Europe and Rest of the World. I used to quote not actual figures, but instead just say that I would charge the exact cost of postage whatever it turned out to be, and not ask any extra for 'handling'. But this was a mistake. Not knowing the cost of postage will put off some buyers and there's nothing wrong with making a small profit on postage to cover your time. It's the people who charge a significant margin above their actual costs who are the gougers, or rip-off merchants.

Note that you are bound by the price that you put on your listing. Note also that buyers who discover that the seller has significantly overcharged on their actual cost for postage and packing have been known to leave negative feedback. For more advice on postage and packing see the 'What to do when you've made your first sale' section on page 99.

Payment methods

If you are willing to sell abroad, you really have to use PayPal – the only issue is whether to accept credit cards or not (see the section 'To PayPal or not to PayPal' starting on page 121). If you're only willing to sell to UK customers, accepting cheques, postal orders and banker's drafts should do. I usually add 'well-concealed cash (at sender's risk)' but it's always overseas buyers who use this option (it can be a useful way to pick up holiday euros). There are other systems, like Bidpay and the like, but they haven't taken off. Since eBay took over PayPal, they have made it an integral part of the way the site works. Having PayPal will increase your number of bidders but you don't have to use it straight away. You can opt in at any time.

eBay also allows you to use **Escrow** – a system whereby the buyer pays money into trust until they have received the goods from the seller. Escrow is not heavily used but might be worth considering for particularly valuable items or if the other party's feedback leaves you in doubt as to whether to deal with them. If they refuse to accept it, that's a good reason not to deal with them and gives you a convincing comeback should they give you negative feedback. There are several reputable Escrow services. They're not cheap. Beware of fraudulent sites.

The auction begins

When you get to the end of the listing process, a message like the one below appears. You will also get an email confirming your listing for each item you list.

Fig 32. Completion of the listing process

During the auction

Watching your own auctions can be entertaining – or dispiriting, if you get no bids until the last day, or even none at all. If you've used a counter (see page 90), you'll be able to tell how many people have looked at your item. If you discover a mistake on your listing you can revise the listing and, provided there are no bids and you haven't gone for the maximum length, you can extend the length of your auction. You can even, as the example I'm about to give shows, change the starting bid or the 'Buy It Now' price.

You can also end your auction early (though you still have to pay eBay's fees), but you have to give a reason for doing so. If you end the auction early but there's already a bidder, there could be recriminations, for obvious reasons. You cannot bid on your own auctions, for equally obvious reasons. If you get somebody else to bid on your auctions, trying to raise the proxy bid of another bidder ('shill bidding') and get caught, you could end up being 'NARU'd'. We'll deal with this further in section 10 on fraud.

When the auction ends

If there are no bidders for your item, you will be given an opportunity to relist it automatically. There are rarely any financial incentives to relist, so it's probably not a good idea. Save your money and work out if you did anything wrong. Was the starting bid too high? Is there only limited demand for what you were selling? Think carefully before you decide whether it's worth listing the item again.

If the item has sold – no matter what the price – you should contact the buyer as quickly as possible. Quite often, they will contact you first, or even pay at once using eBay's checkout system. Make sure you thank them for their business and give clear information on when the item will be sent. There's much more detail in the next section: 'What to do when you've made your first sale.' Now it's time for another case history.

'Dan Dare' - a case history

I'm looking for something to sell that I can use as an example in this book. The other day, while browsing eBay's comics category, I happened to spot a Dan Dare book I have a copy of, *Solid Space Mystery*, and clicked on the 'Add to watch list' link. Now I check how much it went for: £45. Given that this is a book I paid no more than £13 for, this would represent a fair profit after owning it for eight years. There's another copy on offer, currently at £22. I watch that auction too.

I own six Dan Dare books and decide to sell two of them. When I pull them out the tops are dust-encrusted so I have to blow, open and close them, then work very carefully with a tissue to ensure that the dust leaves no stain whatsoever. Three I definitely want to keep. Two are tatty reading copies and I want to hold on to at least one of the hardbacks, so I choose to save the one with the best story. That leaves the last two volumes of the mid-90s hardback reprint books – beautiful books, but the stories in them aren't much cop. One of them is *Solid Space Mystery*, the other *The Final Volume*. There's a bookmark in *The Final Volume* less than a quarter of the way into the book. I never read any further. So that will definitely go. There are none on sale at the moment on eBay but I do a 'completed items' search. One sold five days ago for £44. Promising.

There's a third item I'm not sure whether to sell or not. It's a few years earlier and not a reprint as such, but a book about Dan Dare, from the same publisher, in a slightly smaller format: *Dan Dare Dossier*. It's quite an interesting book, full of archive photos, illustrations and essays, plus a list of every Dan Dare story ever written. If I was a Dan Dare completist, it would be an essential thing to own, but I only own four of this set of books and have barely looked at this one in thirteen years. It's taking up space in one of our most crowded bookshelves. Maybe I can bear to part with it. One page has been miscut and is folded over, but that shouldn't affect the price much. I do a completed items search – there's not been one for sale on eBay recently.

Next, I go to Amazon.co.uk and take a look. Two of their second-hand booksellers have copies of *Dan Dare Dossier*. The first is asking £87.50 for a copy in only 'very good' condition. Mine is at least 'excellent'. There's a single copy that Amazon links to on abebooks.com, the best (but by no means the cheapest) site to find any book on the internet. One of the booksellers on there has a single copy in excellent condition going for . . . wait for it . . . £147.50.

I go to this bookseller's site. The copy of the *Dossier* has been sold (abebooks.com is often out of date but, for once, this is useful to me). However, I see that he has the other two books I've decided to sell, and he's asking £75 each for them. If I put my Dan Dare books up for sale, this shop, or one like it, may well end up buying the books off me and reselling them at a large profit. But, hey, that's capitalism. I decide to go for it.

Listing *The Final Volume*

I start by listing *The Final Volume*. The first stage is to choose a category for the book. I go to the 'Sell Your Item: Select Category' page (if you've forgotten what this looks like, have a look at page 78) and hit the first line 'Click to select' which takes me to categories I've sold in before (eBay is very efficient at remembering your previous preferences). But I've only sold individual, post-1980 comics, so this is no good.

I enter 'eagle comics dan dare' in the search box (I could have got round this by seeing what categories the other sellers used, but at least one of them had listed it as a book for 9-12 year olds – older than I was when I first read the *Eagle* and about forty years younger than the average collector today!). And guess what, there's a category called: 'Books, Comics & Magazines: Comics: UK Comics: Eagle/Dan Dare' so I click on the button that says 'Sell in this category'.

I'm offered the opportunity to sell in another category too, but I suspect this is a waste of money so press the 'Continue' button. I choose a title for my auction, putting the word Dare in twice for emphasis and rewriting a brief description of the first book I want to sell, carefully listing two very minor flaws.

> Dan Dare 12 Dare: The Final Volume HB First
>
> The famous British Dan Dare comic strip ran in the *Eagle* from 1950 to 1967. Hawk published a wonderful facsimile edition, in 12 volumes in the mid-90s, of all but a few of these classic adventures. (The missing adventures, listed in volume 12, from late in the run, have been left out because they were in black and white, or in an unsuitable format, as the *Eagle* messed about with the strip in its later life.) All are out of print and the later ones are hard to find. This copy is unread, in excellent, near mint condition with just a tiny scuff mark on the bottom front left of the cover and a little scuffing at the bottom of the spine. Contents: 'All Treens Must Die'; 'The Mushroom'; 'The Moonsleepers'; 'The Menace From Mars' and 'Operation Moss'.
>
> First edition. ISBN 1899441255
>
> Feel free to ask questions and look out for my other auctions, including the ultra rare '**Dan Dare Dossier**'!

I use a little HTML to put the last three words in bold, a trick I'll explain later. On the next page, I have to choose a starting bid. I select £14.99, as the insertion fee rises from 35p to 75p after that, and I'd still be making a small profit at that price.

Then I have to decide whether to add a 'Buy It Now' option to my auction. I've had some success with this before – impatient buyers will sometimes pay more than the likely final price in order to ensure that they get the item. As soon as somebody bids, though, the 'Buy It Now' option ends and I've wasted the additional fee (that said, I've known an item where somebody has bid low to get rid of the 'Buy It Now' then seen themselves forced to go way above the 'Buy It Now' price to secure the item). Optimistically, I put the BIN at £60.

I have an image of *The Final Volume* cover on my desktop already. By pressing the 'Browse' button I get eBay to find my picture. The box says it may take several minutes to load, but it takes less than one. Then all I have to decide is what to do about postage. I have a look in the free book that any Post Office gives out listing all prices and decide against offering some fancy next-day insured delivery option. Instead I go for the cheapest postage rate I've seen anyone else offering on one of these books: £6.

'I accept PayPal, UK cheques and well-concealed cash (at sender's risk). Postage £6 plus 64p for recorded delivery if required in UK. £9 abroad (large, heavy book). See my other auctions. No extra postage charge for second book.'

The last bit sugars the postage pill if somebody buys more than one of my Dare books. I toy briefly with paying an extra 15p to add a gallery listing, which does exactly what it says in the box below, but decide that it's a needless expense – anyone interested in this book will click on my item. There aren't so many Dare items on sale that I need mine to stand out.

Fig 33. Gallery listings

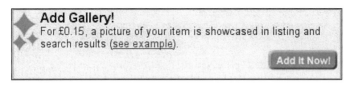

Listing *Solid Space Mystery*

For *The Final Volume* I chose a 10-day auction, but for *Solid Space Mystery* I decide on a 7-day auction. I'd like this auction to end early on Sunday evening, a day before the *The Final Volume*. I'll be out at that time this coming Sunday, so, for convenience, I pay an extra 12p for a scheduled listing.

I change the photograph, but leave the starting bid and 'Buy It Now' price the same at £14.99 and £60 respectively, then finish and log off. The first auction cost me 41p in fees (35p basic listing + 6p BIN), the second 53p (35p + 6p + 12p scheduled listing). Now I just have to wait and see.

Using a counter

I always put a counter on my auctions. It's free, it takes only a single click on the item description page, and it's useful knowing how many people have visited your auction. (The information is available to all users so it can be helpful to a bidder deciding their tactics, too!) Three different styles are offered. The Andale style counter that I prefer looks like this:

Free Counters powered by Andale!

Listing *Dan Dare Dossier*

On Sunday, I decide to list the third book, *Dan Dare Dossier*. Before doing so, I check how my auctions on the first two books are doing, and see that twelve people have visited my auction for *The Final Volume*, but nobody has snapped it up yet on 'Buy It Now'. I decide that the 'Buy It Now' price I've listed is too high and that I need to change it.

Revising items is easy

If I go to an auction I'm running, eBay recognises me, and offers three options: 'Revise your item', 'Promote your item' and 'Sell a similar item'.

Fig 34. Revising items

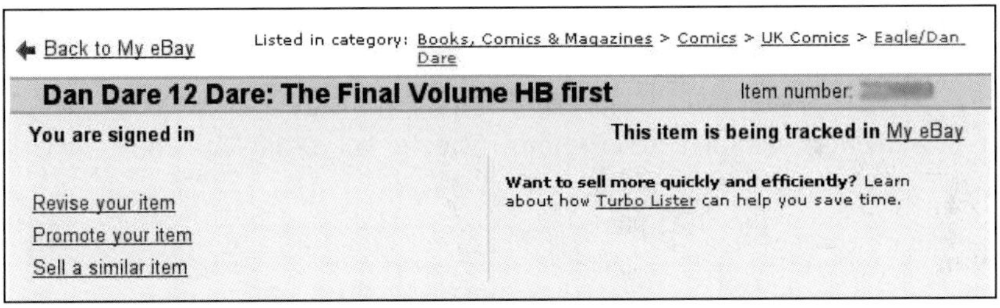

← Back to My eBay	Listed in category: Books, Comics & Magazines > Comics > UK Comics > Eagle/Dan Dare
Dan Dare 12 Dare: The Final Volume HB first	Item number: ███████
You are signed in	This item is being tracked in My eBay
Revise your item Promote your item Sell a similar item	Want to sell more quickly and efficiently? Learn about how Turbo Lister can help you save time.

I click on 'Revise your item' and reduce the 'Buy It Now' on both *The Final Volume* and *Solid Space Mystery* to £50. That's 30p more than a copy of *Solid Space Mystery* went for the day before.

Now I can return to listing *Dan Dare Dossier*. Using 'Sell a similar item' I list it with a starting bid of £29.99 (just below the next fee threshold) and a 'Buy It Now' of £90. Then I sit back to watch all three auctions for the next week.

I'm half expecting somebody to make a low bid to wipe out the 'Buy It Now'. That's a common tactic if somebody really wants an item but thinks the 'Buy It Now' price is more than it will go for. As I explained earlier, BIN-stomping stops an impulse buyer from snapping it up because, once a bid (however low) has been received, the 'Buy It Now' option vanishes. I check the counter a couple of times (eBay only recognises new visitors, so my repeat visits to the page don't add to the Andale tally). Slow but steady traffic.

Disaster!

The following morning, I check one of my favourite sites, NME.com. There's no new music news but, as always when I click on this site, there's one of those annoying pop-up ads for eBay's gallery feature. Normally I get rid of it, but out of curiosity, I type in 'Dan Dare' and click on 'in UK only' to narrow the search. My books don't come up (remember, I didn't pay the extra 15p for a gallery listing) but loads of others do – Dan Dare annuals and dolls. I

> "BIN-stomping stops an impulse buyer from snapping up an item because once a bid has been received, the 'Buy It Now' option vanishes."

go down the page and there, to my annoyance, are no fewer than two copies of *Dan Dare Dossier* and one of the final Dare books. Not only that, but they're all going for less than my starting bids!

I open multiple windows to view these auctions. They're from three different sellers, all with 100 percent feedback records. Each have similar titles to mine, but provide less detailed descriptions. They're all 5-day auctions, two of which were started after mine (which is why I didn't spot them, plus, remember, searches can take a few hours to show up) but will end before mine. I'd be surprised if the seller hadn't checked out my auctions and carefully undercut them. Their postage price is £1 below mine. One has given his starting bid on the *Dossier* as £8.50 and it's already up to £16. He's listed his book as being in 'acceptable' condition, whatever that means. The other has a £20 starting bid which has already been made. It's in 'good' condition. Mine is better than both, but I can see I've overpriced myself. *The Final Volume* is only at £5, but it has a reserve, so may well be more expensive than mine to obtain. It's described as in 'absolutely lovely condition but has been read'. I do a full search. Nobody else is selling *Solid Space Mystery*.

What should I do? The first thing is to click on 'Watch this item in My eBay' so that I can access the latest auction prices on 'My eBay' without having to bookmark the individual items. The next is to decide whether to pull my auctions. It's obvious that I wasn't the only person to notice the high price these books have been going for. There could be a glut of them waiting to leave dusty bookshelves all over the country. I decide not to quit. I'd forfeit my listing fees and I have set the starting bids at the minimum I'd be willing (if unhappy) to accept.

> "The longer you've been on eBay, the more likely you are to use an automatic sniping programme."

Also, if there is a glut, the flood has yet to begin and prices could decline further. I could shorten my auctions, but don't see any advantage in that.

Since there have been no bids on my *Dan Dare Dossier*, and the auction has more than twelve hours to run, I can revise whatever I want. I decide to leave it, knowing there will be no bids until the other auctions finish. This takes away some of the auction's entertainment value. It's fun to check the bids on each of your auctions every day or more often.

My initial optimism has abated. I'm reminded of another lesson about eBay – the first people to sell something can do very well because the item's real rarity value isn't known. But the people who come after inevitably compete to bring the price down.

The first bid

For a couple of days, there's no action on my auctions. On the third day, each book has been viewed just over twenty times, and I get my first bid. Somebody with a positive rating of 261 (and no negatives) has met the high starting bid on *Dan Dare Dossier* and it stands at £29.99. I check on the other two copies of the *Dossier* (which are in inferior condition to mine) and they still stand at £16 and £20, so this bidder must be a serious collector – or, equally likely, a rare book dealer looking for a bargain . . .

I go to London for a couple of days and, when I get back, find I've lost an auction I really wanted to win . . . outbid by fifty cents. I'm beginning to think that I should invest in a sniping programme. According to a book I was reading on the train, the longer you've been on eBay, the more likely you are to use an automatic sniping programme. I check on my Dan Dare books, not expecting anything, and discover that each book is now at the starting bid.

But will they go any higher? The other *Dan Dare Dossiers* on offer are still at prices way below my starting bid of £29.99.

The next afternoon, with two days to go on two of the auctions, I do my daily check. The first *Dan Dare Dossier* to sell has gone for £45. The other is still at £22, while mine remains at the starting bid of £29.99. My copy of *The Final Volume* is now up to £22. The other auction for *The Final Volume*, which ends soon, is at £26.33. My copy of *Solid Space Mystery* is at £26.33.

Fig 35. Update on the auction for *Solid Space Mystery*

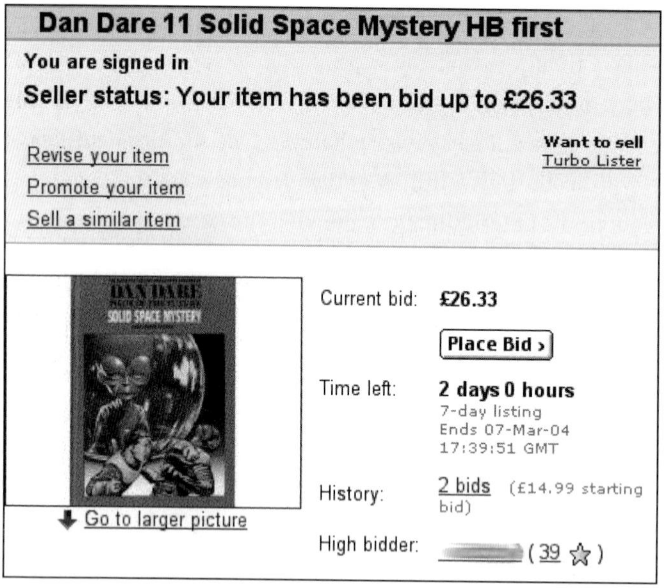
Dan Dare 11 Solid Space Mystery HB first
You are signed in
Seller status: Your item has been bid up to £26.33
Want to sell
Turbo Lister
Revise your item
Promote your item
Sell a similar item
Current bid: £26.33
Place Bid ›
Time left: 2 days 0 hours
7-day listing
Ends 07-Mar-04
17:39:51 GMT
History: 2 bids (£14.99 starting bid)
High bidder: (39 ☆)
Go to larger picture

This unusual figure tells me, without looking at the bidding history, that the same bidders are going for these books. The one who has been outbid had a high bid of £25.33. I don't know what the current high bidder's top proxy price is, but he's been forced to pay £1 more than the highest bid of the first bidder. The auctions are starting to get interesting. I'll look back more often over the next two days. And, remember, most bids take place during the closing seconds.

Next day, with thirty hours to go, there are no more bids on my auctions. Of the other sales going on, the first *Dan Dare Dossier* ('good condition and will ship to UK only') went for £31.06, only a little over my starting bid. The other copy of *The Final Volume* ('excellent conditon') went for £36. I can expect no more than this for my copy, probably less. The 'acceptable condition' *Dossier* went for £45.10. So I'll be unhappy if I get less than this for mine. Today, another copy went on sale, in slightly better condition than mine. The seller has put the starting bid at £35. This too, could affect my final price. The knowledge that there's still another one on sale might stop some bidders going as high as they otherwise would.

A couple of hours later I check and the high bid on my copy of *Solid Space Mystery* has gone up to £32.05, thanks to a second bid by the first bidder. So now I know that the second bidder's maximum was £31.05 (at over £30, the bid increment was £1, though it has since gone up). This bidder is now the high bidder on two of my three auctions. Possibly he's tempted by my postage offer (remember, I said there would be no extra charge if the buyer wins more than one book).

With just over an hour to go, there's a fourth bidder on *Solid Space Mystery*. The price has risen to £33.05, so the previous price must have been the buyer's maximum. It's the last bid. My copy of the *Dan Dare Dossier*, meanwhile, goes to a US buyer for the opening bid of £29.99. Disappointing.

There are no snipes on the first two auctions.

Getting paid

Using the 'Send an invoice' button on my item page, I contact the buyers, asking how they want to pay. This automatically gives me the buyers' addresses (getting the addresses without an email from the buyer can be tricky, as we shall see). In the morning, one has replied that he will send me a personal cheque.

My third auction – for *The Final Volume* – ends with a last-minute snipe, taking the price from £22 to £26.33 and the buyer pays instantly. This costs me £1.38 in final value fees (5.25% x £26.33) as the PayPal screen overleaf shows.

Fig 36. eBay transaction summary and statement of fees

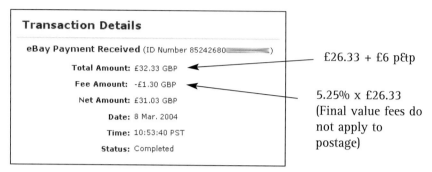

Annoyingly, this instant payment makes it hard for me to find his address. I pull the buyer's contact details from eBay. Oddly, these include his phone number but not his address (eBay seems to assume that you have the address). Then I go through the PayPal site and discover his address beneath the payment details shown above. Sorted. The cheque comes by first post the next day. I double wrap the two paid-for books in bubble wrap and heavy-duty Jiffy bags and take them to the Post Office.

I'd charged six pounds postage for each – a guess, and, as it turns out, a good one. The cheaper book is the heavier one, too heavy to go first class. I pay £6.55 for Special Delivery, which guarantees that it will arrive within 24 hours. The other costs £5.45 for first class, so I've broken even on the postage. The Special Delivery is insured. I get a proof of posting slip for the other, which is therefore only covered up to £28. I'll bear the extra £5.05 risk myself.

Next day, the first buyer contacts me, saying he's delighted with the speed of the delivery and is sending me the extra postage cost. I tell him there's no need to bother and he leaves the following feedback:

Comment	From
🟢 A*** Brilliant !! How all ebay traders should be.	Buyer

Sure enough, two days later, I get 70p in the post, a reminder that most eBayers pride themselves on the fairness that the community approach encourages. On the other hand, I still haven't heard from my American buyer, but I'm not worried. He has a positive feedback rating of 258 with no negatives and only one neutral.

Three days have passed since the sale, though, so on Thursday morning I decide to take the next step: a payment reminder. I mean to use the official form for this which you can find on the original item page. Alternatively, I could go through my bookmarked 'eBay items I'm selling' page and adjust the preference panel to show items I've sold in the last four days rather than the default position, which is two. But while I'm doing this, I download my emails and there, sent just within the three day limit, is a PayPal payment (curiously, the American form does include the buyer's address, unlike the UK one) with a polite note thanking me for the book I'm about to send.

All three sales have ended with the minimum of hassle. The prices were disappointing (eBay claims that items with Gallery listings sell for twenty percent more, on average, so maybe I made a mistake there), but still more than twice what I paid for the books in the first place, and I've gained some shelf space. My total eBay fees were £6.37 and I also had to give PayPal £3.02 (note that PayPal, unlike eBay, takes a slice of the postage fee too) for the two payments I received through them. Since eBay owns PayPal, they took a total of £9.39 on transactions worth a total of £89.37 (excluding postage fees), not far short of eleven percent. That's how eBay makes its money.

Summary of eBay fees on my Dan Dare books

	Final Vol. listed at £14.99 sold for £26.33	SS Mystery listed at £14.99 sold for £33.05	DD Dossier listed at £29.99 sold for £29.99
Listing	£0.35	£0.35	£0.75
BIN	£0.06	£0.06	£0.06
Scheduled	–	£0.12	–
Final value	£1.38	£1.67	£1.57
Total	£1.79	£2.20	£2.38

What to do when you've made your first sale

Contacting the buyer

Your first successful auction is over and now you have to complete the deal. eBay allows buyer and seller up to three days to contact each other, but it looks best if you contact the buyer within 24 hours and certainly by the end of the next working day (though bear in mind time differences and that every other first world country has more public holidays than the UK).

If you've arranged your auction to end around a time when you're on the computer, you can contact the buyer straight away, congratulating them on winning the auction and asking how they want to pay. Note, though, that if you've decided to take PayPal, the logo that appears on your auction will allow the buyer to click through and pay straight away. If the buyer's been waiting for the auction to end, they may make an online payment very soon after the auction's end, saving you time. So there's no need to rush to send out the bill. It may not be necessary.

In the UK, buyers often send cheques. Whether you wait for the cheque to clear or not is a judgement call. Your decision will probably rest on the amount at stake, and how good the buyer's feedback is. If the amount's modest, and the buyer has good feedback, I cash the cheque and post the item the same day, with an email to the effect that I'll leave feedback after the cheque's cleared. This generally ensures that the buyer leaves me good feedback. I've never been ripped off. However, you may regard this as an unacceptable risk. (Note that cheques can take a long time to finish clearing or bounce, and read the warning on cheque scams in the final section of this book.)

What happens when the buyer breaks the rules

In my early days on eBay, I assumed it wasn't worth selling cheaper items abroad, because of the high postage costs, and when I listed them I always put 'UK and Europe only'. How wrong I was. A large proportion of US sellers won't sell to anyone outside the US but US buyers, I found, blithely ignored my 'UK and Europe' only stipulation. I could have cancelled their bids, though, as a newbie, I didn't know that this was an option. I could have refused to sell them the goods and sold to the next highest bidder (this is possible, but the process is a pain). But, instead, I tried to make the deals work. If the buyer wanted to pay in cash, and didn't have access to UK funds, I accepted dollars, but charged an extra $3 as a contribution to my exchange costs. (The banks' minimum fee at the time was around £5.) I saved up dollars to exchange in a big wad, but usually ended up sending them back across the ocean to pay for an auction I'd won.

Postage and packing

The key points where postage and packing are concerned are transparency over costs and properly protecting the goods being sent. If you're only charging for the actual amount of postage, it's acceptable to use packing materials that are being reused for the umpteenth time, as long as they thoroughly protect whatever it is you're sending. But if you're marking up your prices to cover the cost of your time and packaging the item, you should make sure that the packaging looks smart as well as efficient. I'm not saying 'don't use recycled packaging' – I invariably do and have never had an objection.

You should always charge exactly what it says on your item description. When you complete the 'Sell an item' form, eBay says that you are entitled to charge more to overseas bidders and does not insist that you specify the amount. That said, it makes sense to give a cost, rounding it up to be sure you're not out of pocket.

In my early selling days, I used to specify that I charged the actual shipping price only, but this was a mistake for at least three reasons. First, I had to make a special trip to the Post Office to ascertain how much it would cost me, for instance, to post an LP to Japan. Secondly, the lack of information about the postage cost may have put off some buyers. Finally, waiting to work out postage costs delays the buyer's ability to pay you, which is bad business.

If you're willing to sell abroad but can't be bothered to work out a price for every region, the standard way of dealing with the situation is to use wording like 'overseas bidders, email for the cost of posting to your region before bidding'. If you do this, make sure you're in a position to reply within a day or so.

The kind of packaging you use will depend on the item you're selling. Lightweight mailers such as Jiffy bags will cover all kinds of things but may not be appropriate for fragile or heavy items (CD cases are notoriously easy to break, but Jiffy bags seem less prone to cracked cases than the cardboard cases that some CD sites use). For extremely fragile items your buyer may insist on a particular form of protection, but this should be agreed before the sale. Never allow

> "The key points where postage and packing are concerned are transparency over costs and properly protecting the goods being sent."

fragile items to touch each other inside a packet or carton, for obvious reasons. You can use a box within a box for fragile items, but bear in mind the total weight and use lightweight packaging where appropriate.

For items that need to be kept flat like, say, collectable comics, vinyl records or sheet music, use rigid packaging rather than padded envelopes (or if you use a padded envelope, put cardboard stiffeners inside). Mark the item 'do not bend' as well as, if appropriate, using a 'fragile' sticker. **Don't overprotect your item by, for example, using endless quantities of sticky tape.** It should be possible to open the package easily. Bear in mind that not all buyers have agile, strong hands or someone to help them.

Padded envelopes are especially important for items with odd shapes or sharp edges. The Post Office will give you blue-on-white 'Fragile' stickers to put on the outside of your item if appropriate. Always cover any sharp staple edges with tape. Always put your return address on the outside of the packet (one time I didn't, just after the post 9/11 anthrax scare in the US and the packet took three months to arrive – luckily, it was to a friend, not an eBayer). Many sellers also include a print-out of the relevant email exchanged about the transaction or, at least, the item number.

Make the most of the Royal Mail

The Royal Mail publishes a booklet which explains its basic services. It's updated about once a year. If you're going to sell at all regularly, it's well worth getting one of these booklets (they're free from Post Offices and the current one is headed: 'Our Services - All You Need To Know').

The booklet has a long section on wrapping and packing. It also includes information on insurance and compensation, plus the cost of sending anything First Class, Second Class or Parcel Post. It explains Recorded Delivery and Special Delivery and how long mail takes to reach other countries. And, I stress, it's free.

I'm not a huge fan of the Royal Mail, especially since it closed the Post Office branch at the bottom of my road, but it's likely to be your first port of call.

If you're thinking of selling something that requires more specialised delivery, like a courier service, see what your competitors do, and how much they charge to do it. Bear in mind, by the way, that the Royal Mail packing instructions are partly designed to cover the Royal Mail. For instance, I have never come across any seller who puts 2cm of soft wrapping around every CD case, as the booklet recommends (although that could be why so many arrive broken).

By the way, there's a useful discussion board on postage and packing on eBay.co.uk which you can get to from the site map. You can find postage fees and a list of available services on the Royal Mail website at:

- www.royalmail.com

If you become a heavy eBay seller, it might be worth using the SmartStamp scheme, which allows you to print off your own prepaid postage. Otherwise, if you get in a supply of stamps in various denominations and use a set of kitchen scales, you can avoid trips to the Post Office for items that will fit in a postbox (note that most Post Offices will happily give you a supply of 'fragile' and 'airmail' stickers).

Insurance

Some sellers charge insurance but don't actually have any insurance arrangements in place. If an item goes missing, they say they'll bear the cost themselves. This is fraudulent. You might want to use the Royal Mail insurance service or another such, but bear in mind that you're entitled to compensation of up to £28 for mail that goes missing anyway, provided you can prove the value (maximum compensation is only £20 for parcels and, in each case, the amount is 'or the market value, whichever is lower'). Some sellers have been known to charge for 'insurance' when all they have in place is the standard Post Office compensation. This is also fraudulent, but is unlikely to land them in trouble.

In order to get compensation, should anything go wrong, it's essential that, whenever you're sending anything that's been bought on eBay, **you always get a proof of posting form**. These can be obtained when you're paying at the Post Office counter. Usually the Post Office gets you to fill in the address yourself, then stamps the form. Some Post Offices will fill out the form for you. Either way, you can prove that you sent an item to the address of the buyer. I've never had to use a proof of posting form as proof of an eBay transaction, but there's always a first time (note: many Post Offices now use receipts that, when filled in, double as a proof of posting form).

Problems after posting

When the item has been sent to the winning buyer, I generally tell them that it's on the way and that I've left feedback (you may not want to do this, for reasons already discussed). Often the only way that you find out the item has been received is when you see the feedback that the buyer in turn has left for you. Don't be upset if the buyer doesn't leave positive feedback. Between a quarter and a third of buyers don't leave feedback and it's definitely not worth chasing. Let it go.

If a buyer has problems (like the article not arriving, or arriving damaged) they should let you know as soon as possible. It's your job to put the situation right. Remember, eBay is the venue but you're one of the parties to the transaction. You have to act responsibly. What follows is a rough rule of thumb for dealing with the main problems. Bear in mind that most of these problems are fairly rare.

Item not as described

If the buyer claims that the article is not as you described it, either because it is not the item they thought they were buying, or it is not in the condition that they were led to expect, you should try to resolve the situation amicably. If they're plainly wrong, resist the temptation to be rude. Most likely, they have misread your item description in some respect. Simply point out what was said in the original item description and offer to refund their payment (but not post and packing) if they return the item to you. That way, you're both out equal amounts of post and packing and you can reclaim your fees from eBay or sell to the next highest bidder. It's a pain but, in most cases, especially if it's an inexpensive item, simply making the offer will mollify the buyer and end the problem.

If the buyer is right, you should bend over backwards to rectify the situation. Offer a partial refund or full refund if they want to return the item. Explain the cause of the mistake if you can. If there's an honest disagreement about some aspect of condition, try to reach a compromise. I've only once had this situation where, after buying a record on the 'Buy It Now' option, a buyer asked for clarification about its condition, using a term I'd never heard before ('ring wear' – it describes the mark left on the sleeve by the central section of a record: and there was a slight ring wear mark on this sleeve). Arguably, by asking after buying, the buyer had forfeited the right to complain, but I knocked a small amount off the price and he left me great feedback.

Item doesn't arrive

Until the item reaches the buyer, you're responsible for it. If the item doesn't arrive, you, not the buyer, have to claim at the Post Office. Always assume that the buyer is telling the truth and use your common sense as to when to send a refund. It's probably best to do this rather more quickly than the Royal Mail will reimburse you for lost items.

If you think that you're a victim of attempted fraud, look at the section which starts on page 137 of this book. As with most things in life, it's prudent to act on the assumption that the other party is acting with the best of intentions. If you haven't taken out insurance and the item value exceeds the Post Office's maximum compensation, you're in trouble. Remember that items do get delayed in the post, especially abroad (Canada seems to be particularly bad for this) so don't rush to return the buyer's money.

Communication is of key importance. Rapid replies and clear correspondence give the buyer and seller confidence. Most of the time, the missing items show up.

Item arrives damaged

If an item arrives damaged, ask the buyer to hold onto all the packaging as this will be needed for your Post Office compensation claim. If you've obviously packaged an item inadequately, you're going to have to bear the cost of a refund (or a partial one, if the buyer agrees). The buyer might be willing to keep the damaged item if you give them a partial refund – it depends on the buyer and the kind of item. If the Post Office is at fault, the responsibility for arranging compensation is yours, not the buyer's. You can get a leaflet at the Post Office or phone their customer services on 08457 740740 (calls charged at local rate).

One final word on this – it's not worth getting paranoid about packaging or delivery problems and insuring yourself up to your eyeballs. If you're selling very valuable items overseas, it can be worth offering online tracking and insurance (if the buyer doesn't accept these options, then they, at the very least, share responsibility for any loss). Bear in mind that:

- the majority of people are honest, especially when dealing with individuals rather than institutions; and
- the Post Office delivers to 27 million addresses every day. There are lots of horror stories about stolen and undelivered mail. Some sorting offices do seem to have severe problems at the time of writing. Nevertheless, only a miniscule proportion of deliveries fail to get to their destination in the condition in which they were sent.

Keep good records

Selling on eBay is a hobby and a business, so it behoves you to keep records of every transaction up to and beyond the point where both parties have left feedback. Create a folder in your email programme for all of your eBay emails and, as a back-up, I suggest you keep a paper folder with all correspondence, postage receipts and so on.

There is a second practical reason for keeping good records: should your eBay trading take off, and become something big enough for the Inland Revenue to consider a business, you will need to have good records. However, your main concern should be to be in a position where you can get the details of any transaction easily and quickly. How long to keep these records for is another matter. If you're not building a business, so don't need tax records or the ability to target former buyers, then throw all but the most recent stuff out once a year and start again.

Some guidance on the tax implications of eBay trading is provided in Appendix 6 on page 175, but if your trading starts to get serious (i.e. frequent and high-value) you'd be well-advised to get professional advice from an accountant.

Advanced
buying and selling

● ●

Auction or 'Buy It Now'?

We've already talked about whether you should include a 'Buy It Now' price with your auction, but here we'll discuss it a little further, along with the more vexed question of whether you should have a 'Buy It Now-*only*' sale instead of an auction.

BIN-only sales account for a relatively small proportion of sales on eBay and, as they aren't auctions, it could be argued that they don't belong in this book. But they're an option. Are they an option worth considering? Definitely.

The thing is, some buyers prefer the certainty of fixed sale prices, particularly when it comes to buying presents at Christmas, where buyers don't have time to wait for an auction to end. Indeed, eBay's research has shown that some buyers don't like auctions, full stop. They like certainty, or they just don't have a lot of time to spend online. Also, according to auction theory, auctions aren't the most efficient means of selling goods where the final price is predictable. They involve too much effort for both buyer and seller.

In what circumstances, then, might you want to sell items in a BIN-only sale rather than in an auction? I can think of a few:

- If you're hoping for a **quick** sale on an item.
- If you're selling the sort of item where buyers are likely to want it **straight away**, at a price low enough that they aren't tempted to chase an auction to save a few pennies or cents.

- If you're selling **multiple copies** of the same item (note: you have to pay a listing fee for each copy you're selling, so don't go crazy with the quantity).

Even so, many sellers prefer the 'auction *with* Buy It Now' route, putting a lower starting bid and counting on the market to set a price that often works out a little below the BIN price. If a bidder can't wait, they can buy it straight away.

There are times when having an 'auction with BIN' can hurt you. If you list something that you don't know the true value of and set the BIN price too low, a collector is likely to snap it up before the auction process has time to set a fair price, and you lose out.

BIN-stomping

Set your starting bid low but with a high 'Buy It Now' and you risk being BIN-stomped – somebody bids your minimum purely in order to get rid of the BIN option, hoping to get the item for less than it is worth.

Some sellers complain about this, but I don't see the problem. You set your starting bid at the minimum you're willing to accept – if you make this ridiculously low, that's because you're hoping the extra bidders who come in will end up forcing the price higher. If you really want the BIN price and aren't willing to take less, you should make yours a BIN-only sale.

From the stomper's point of view, what BIN-stomping does is eliminate the risk of somebody paying the high BIN price, giving the stomper time to decide if they really want the item at a time nearer to the end of the auction. They risk the price going higher than the BIN price, but, presumably, they wouldn't have paid that price anyhow, so won't lose out.

I've had BINs removed by a lowish first bid, then seen the price rise higher than the BIN price. I've also set what I thought were unrealistic BIN prices and seen them met by buyers not willing to risk another buyer beating them to the item. That's what makes BIN an interesting addition to the eBay experience – it's like adding a wild card to a poker game: unpredictable and exciting. Sometimes you win. Sometimes you lose.

Unofficial 'Buy It Nows'

It's possible that, as a seller, when there are no bids and you don't have a 'Buy It Now' (or even when there are bids and/or the BIN has been stomped), you will be approached to end the auction early at a price agreed between buyer and seller and complete the transaction outside eBay. It's impossible to know how often this happens. Should you go for this deal, you wouldn't get feedback or fraud protection and risk being NARU'd (see the 'Feedback' section which starts on page 61).

Ending auctions early

If you need to end an auction early, go to the 'End my listing early' link on the site map and follow the instructions there. Note that **you have to give a reason for ending the auction** and this has changed since the first edition of this book. Ending auctions early for non-valid reasons (like illness or changing your mind) is against eBay's rules. Valid reasons are that the item is no longer for sale, the item is lost or broken, an error in the listing or an error in the starting price or reserve amount. If you have bids on your listing, or if the reserve price has been met, you must cancel all bids or sell to the high bidder, rather than end the auction). If you cancel bids, you risk complaints against you from the disappointed bidders. So it's not advisable to end an auction early unless you've had no bids. It is no longer possible to cancel an auction in the last twelve hours if you have a bidder (unless you sell to that bidder). You may block specific bidders but the 'cancel all bids and end this item' feature is now gone.

Bid retraction

It is possible to retract your bid before the auction ends (not afterwards) but, be warned, your number of bid retractions will show up on your feedback page for the next six months. The eBay bid retraction form only offers three reasons for bid retraction:

1. that you entered the wrong amount (if you add an extra digit, you should retract immediately);
2. that the item description has changed significantly; or
3. that you can't contact the seller.

This last is defined as "you tried calling the seller but his or her phone number doesn't work, or you have tried emailing a message to the seller and it comes back undeliverable". The reason for contacting the seller isn't defined, but eBay suggests that if you have a reason for retracting not mentioned above, you should contact the seller and ask them to consider cancelling your bid (see below).

Requesting that the seller cancel your bid is the only course of action open to you should you suddenly lose your job while bidding on a dozen auctions and need to withdraw from them all. If the seller agrees to cancel your bid, this won't count as a retraction and, therefore, won't show up on your feedback. Chances are, if you ask nicely well before the end of the auction, it will work: no seller wants a deadbeat buyer.

Note that you can't withdraw a bid in the last twelve hours of an auction unless the bid was made during that period, in which case you get an hour in which to withdraw. Nor can a seller make any changes to the item description in the last twelve hours. The prohibition of late retractions helps to defeat buyer bid shielding, where the buyer gets a friend to make an artificially high bid just after theirs, then withdraw it just before the auction ends so that the item sells for the (artificially low) previous bid.

> "Be warned, your number of bid retractions will show up on your feedback page for the next six months."

Bid cancellation

A seller has the right to cancel your bid when, for whatever reason, they feel uncomfortable about completing the transaction. This could be because you have poor or negative feedback, live in a country they won't sell to or because you've put 'Adolf Hitler' as your username. If they do this, they will probably put you on their blocked bidders list, too. (If a seller follows eBay's procedures for refund of fees when a buyer fails to complete, the deadbeat buyer will automatically be put on the seller's blocked bidders list.)

Non-paying bidders ('NPBs')

If a buyer doesn't come through with their payment after you've sent a couple of reminders and more than a week has gone by, you can submit a non-paying bidder alert form (note: a week is the minimum wait before giving a warning, 45 days is the maximum – you must request the credit within 60 days of your auction close). Click on 'Request final value fee credit' on the site map. eBay will automatically contact the user warning them that they have been accused of bidding and not paying. If the buyer does not resolve the matter, you will get your eBay final value fee recredited to your account (but not your listing fee). You may also (and usually should) leave negative feedback.

eBay operates a three strikes and you're out policy. You get two warnings for non-payment and, with the third one, an NPB is suspended for thirty days. Should they then fail to pay a third time, they will get an indefinite suspension from eBay. As a seller, you should understand that computers crash, relatives die or have accidents, people get hospitalised, and so on. Therefore, while you should file NPB within a couple of weeks, you might

> "If you sell a lot, you're bound to get some NPBs, but they're often newbies."

want to hold off on the negative feedback. The eBay warning notices give NPBs the chance to appeal if they have extenuating circumstances. If you work things out with your buyer, you should file an NPB Warning Removal within ninety days of the auction end.

If you sell a lot, you're bound to get some NPBs, but they're often newbies (I suspect, from the correspondence, that the ones I've had to deal with were underage users who hit the 'Buy It Now' without clearing it with their parents first).

Using different accounts

If you have more than one non-web-based email address, it is possible to have more than one eBay account (but cookies mean that, if you use the same computer to access all your accounts, eBay will tend to remember you as the last account you used).

There are sellers who have different accounts for each different kind of merchandise they sell. They argue that this allows them to have a different 'About me' page for each kind of merchandise. A more likely rationale is that, if the seller screws up selling one kind of merchandise, the bad feedback won't affect their other selling operations.

It isn't against eBay rules to have more than one account, but it does look suspicious. eBay has software in place that detects different kinds of fraud, including suspicious patterns of buying and selling that could constitute shill bidding (cooperation between accounts to raise or artificially lower the final selling price). If, as a buyer or seller, you use multiple accounts to try and 'fix' auctions, they'll catch up with you sooner or later. The majority of fraudsters are turned in by other eBay users before the software has picked up suspicious patterns.

Favourite stores and searches

If you want to repeat a particular search – advanced or otherwise – the quickest way to do it is still to bookmark the search on your browser. However, if you have half as many bookmarks as I do, you don't want to keep adding new ones, although dividing particular kinds of bookmark into their own folder helps. eBay has a pull down menu that appears on some browsers, showing recent searches and a 'My Favourites' subsection of 'My eBay'. When you do a search, look on the right before you get to the results listing and you'll see:

Fig 37. Link that enables you to add a search to your favourites

■ **Add to Favourites**

Click on this. It will give you the option to be emailed every time a new item matching the search criteria is added to eBay – I wouldn't choose that option unless the item is reasonably specialised or you want it in a real hurry.

The favourites page also offers you the chance to click through your favourite sellers and your favourite categories. It's only the equivalent of having a folder full of bookmarks, but it is convenient and it's just one bookmark to add to the other four I've suggested (the bidding and selling pages of 'My eBay', the site map and the UK homepage). You can also get to it by clicking on 'Favourite searches' in the eBay tool bar.

There's no such thing as a free listings day

Every so often, eBay tries to tempt sellers with special offers. The UK site used to have a free listings day every few months. eBay.co.uk would send emails promoting these to sellers who hadn't placed many auctions lately. More recently, it has offered free listings for items with a start price of under a pound, 'Buy It Now-only' items, car auctions and items that list PayPal as a payment option and are paid for with PayPal. Then there are 5p listings days and other offers designed to promote particular selling features.

Fig 38. Free listing day advert

These incentives are intended to promote the site or new features, but they're not designed to do favours for sellers. Indeed, some experienced sellers avoid putting items up for sale during free listings periods. This is because sellers use free listings days to unload the stuff that they wouldn't normally waste a listing fee on. You also get sellers who are too mean to list at any other time.

Free listings days benefit buyers

Even if you never sell on eBay, it's worth making a note of when there's a free listings day because, in the week to ten days afterwards, there will be increased listings, often from inexperienced sellers. It's a good time to pick up a bargain. There's more stuff around (and more mislabelled goodies, plus items from infrequent sellers who don't know the value of what they've got) so the prices are inevitably lower. They benefit eBay because they get a surge in final value fees from sellers who wouldn't otherwise be selling. But the seller, more often than not, loses out.

When using a free listings day, I keep the starting bids low (and I've been known to lower prices when I see what sells and what doesn't) in the knowledge that it's not costing me anything and I could do with clearing some space (I live in a house overflowing with books and CDs). I've found that, when I list something that is rare and in demand, it gets a good price whether I use a free listings day

> 'Sellers use free listings days to unload the stuff that they wouldn't normally waste a listing fee on.'

or not. Rare, in demand goods will always sell and the period following a free listings (or similar) day may exact a higher price because of all the extra sharks circling the eBay pool in search of a bargain. But if I list something fairly common and the item sells, it generally goes for the starting bid.

I sometimes use free listings days to unload the sort of items – mostly CDs – I'd otherwise put up in the attic because I can't quite bring myself to throw them out. Some of this rubbish sells but at a much lower rate than my normal auctions, often the starting bid. Given the time I've wasted doing the listings, I'd have been better off giving them to a charity shop.

There's always Oxfam

What I don't sell on a free listings day either goes into the attic or is taken to Oxfam (and here let me put in a plug for Oxfam, already the biggest second-hand bookseller in the UK and on its way to being the biggest second-hand music seller in the UK). They have trained graders and, where appropriate, charge collector's prices for books and records. Where appropriate, they even sell on eBay. So, if you've got stuff you can't be bothered to shift on eBay but which is likely to have a market, why not give it to your local branch and help out people less fortunate than yourself. The good buzz it gives you might be worth more than money.

Turbo Lister

eBay's Turbo Lister feature is a free desktop software tool designed to make listing multiple items faster and easier. It allows you to list multiple items all at once and save listings to reuse again and again. If you start selling heavily, it's worth checking out, and more info can be found at:

- pages.ebay.co.uk/turbo_lister/

You can create listings offline, which is handy if you have a metered connection or want to prepare auctions for later and don't want to fork out for a scheduled listing. eBay say that the feature's useful even if you're a relatively low-volume eBay seller. However, like the eBay toolbar, it's not compatible with Mac operating systems, so I don't use it myself.

Tax and VAT issues

If you trade on eBay so much that the taxman takes an interest in what you're doing, you've become a small business and moved beyond the scope of this book. Take a look at the HM Revenue & Customs website at:

- www.hmrc.gov.uk

There's specific information about ecommerce and claiming computer expenses at:

- www.hmrc.gov.uk/e-commerce/sme4a.htm

For most sellers, Customs and Excise (which has now merged with the Inland Revenue) is a bigger issue. You have to fill in a customs form when sending goods abroad. On it you list the contents, value and whether the goods are merchandise or a gift. Sellers abroad have to do the same thing, and they're more than a formality. This is discussed in more depth in Appendix 6 on page 175.

A nasty little surcharge surprise

Value Added Tax is due on all goods imported into the UK, regardless of whether they are new or second-hand. Notice 143, a guide for international post users (March 2002) on the HM Revenue & Customs website explains this in more detail than I have room for here. The general rule appears to be that you will pay VAT at the applicable rate in the UK if the item attracts VAT when new (i.e. DVDs yes, books no) or a 3.5% import duty if VAT doesn't apply, but only if the item costs more than £18 (not including the postage and packing element). If the package is a gift, then you will not be charged unless its value exceeds £36.

In addition to VAT and Customs fees, you may also have to pay the Royal Mail which charges a fee for administering any import duty due. This is currently £4, regardless of the value of the package. eBay advises that you fill in all forms honestly and sellers who are asked to falsify information to save the buyer money may not take kindly to the request. That said, I've found anecdotal evidence to suggest that some sellers, particularly in the US, routinely lower the value of goods on the customs form, even ticking 'gift' rather than 'merchandise' to save the buyer being hit by import taxes. This approach works, at virtually no risk to the seller, if the value of the goods is hard to determine, but HM Revenue & Customs do routinely open packets to check that the contents are what they say they are. The buyer has to pay the fee or refuse their goods.

Some sellers claim that they will pay any Customs fees – this should act as a warning sign that they are blatantly breaking rules and buyers will definitely not be able to hold them to it.

I've only once been hit by a Customs fee. Remember that 'Lost In Translation' DVD I was after earlier in this book? I decided to buy it from Amazon.com. I combined the shipping cost with that of another DVD. Big mistake. I got two

DVDs that weren't released in the UK for less than £12.50 each, but I also had to pay £4 to the Royal Mail and £4.13 to Customs (and drive to the Post Office to collect them). Amazon very clearly lists the content and value of goods in its packages, meaning that Customs almost always collects. So you might want to think carefully before buying items from abroad that cost more than £18, or at least factor the import costs into the equation. For more information, go to the main Customs site at:

- www.hmrc.gov.uk

There is also a Customs guide to trading on the internet at:

- www.hmrc.gov.uk/e-commerce/sme1.htm

Radio Free Europe

I collect CDs, but they're not exactly fetish objects, with their tiny covers and easily cloned contents. My favourite musical fetish is for 7" vinyl singles. I have two record decks and a collection of 2,000 singles or so in the study where I keep my second hi-fi. I no longer collect as exhaustively as I once did, with one exception. My favourite group is REM, who I first saw over twenty years ago at Nottingham's Rock City, with less than a hundred people in the audience. Back then, their first single, 'Radio Free Europe', released on a tiny independent label, Hibtone, had been out less than two years. There are two versions with minor differences and I've never come across a copy. Moreover, the original version of 'Radio Free Europe' and its B side have never been available on CD. My net buddy Hank (see page 149) has one, bought for 75p in 1983 – it's now worth at least two hundred times as much.

I want one. I've bid on the occasional copy over the years but never come close to winning. Recently one in mediocre condition peaked at $71, not meeting its reserve. I went for the one before that, despite it having a slight imperfection on the sleeve. This one went for $127.50, well above my maximum bid of $91. Another copy came up in between those two, but was withdrawn with the first bid at the starting bid, $25. The seller had made a mistake with his picture, posting an Armani shirt instead. Misdescribed items can turn out to be bargains and picture aside, it sounded like a very good copy, so I was interested. Only trouble was, the description said "will post to US only".

I wrote the seller a friendly email asking whether he was willing to post to the UK. He replied that he'd only put 'US only' as this was the default and he was happy to post to me. He then wrote again, saying that he'd been forced to withdraw the auction because pictures can't be changed, but he was about to relist it.

The new listing was much more detailed, full of scans, and mentioned that the last copy in nearly as good condition as his went for $200. He even gave the item code for this copy, so that buyers could check out that he was telling the truth (he was). An advanced search on 'Completed items' for REM Hibtone showed that the copies mentioned above were the only ones to be sold recently. So I bided my time and watched as the bid quickly shot up to $99.50. And stayed there. And stayed there.

The auction ended at 6.43pm on a Saturday, a time when I could be at my computer. I decided to bid in the last few minutes, but not to go over the amount in my PayPal account. I'd won one CD since selling the Dan Dare books and still had £66.40 or $118.74 in the account. So $118.74 became my maximum bid. I waited and waited to put the bid in, but had to allow a few spare seconds in case eBay asked me to retype my password, delaying my bid. It didn't. With 34 seconds to go, I was the high bidder, at $102.50. The bidder before me must have had a maximum of $101.50. Would they bid again? Had someone set a bid with sniping software that would come in during the last few seconds? Nervously, I pressed 'refresh' on my browser. This is what came up:

Fig 39. Congratulations message to winning bidder

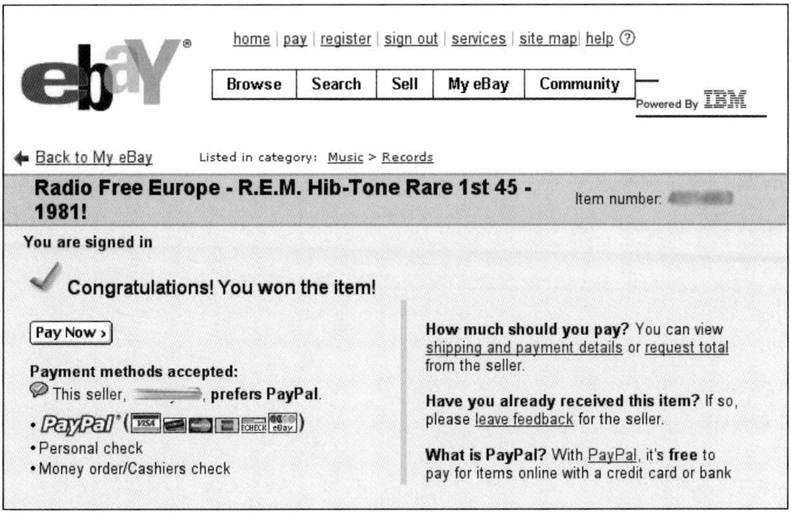

I then had to negotiate the postage method with the seller. This added an extra $13.70 to the cost, still within my budget. By the time the discs were posted, the seller and I had exchanged at least half a dozen emails each and were gossiping about bands we'd seen. Finally, I had a nervous wait to see if the single arrived and whether customs surcharged me.

It did. They didn't.

To PayPal or not to PayPal

● ●

The ability to pay for goods in a speedy online transaction is crucial to trading on the net. Secure server systems mean that it's often safer to use credit cards online than it is in face-to-face transactions where card details can be cloned in seconds. However most individuals aren't empowered to take credit cards. On eBay, where individuals dominate, the need for a quick, easy and safe online payment system for small sellers was spotted by many, including eBay itself, which bought the Billpoint payment site.

The online payment service PayPal began operations in October 1999. It wasn't intended for use in auctions, but this quickly became what is known as its 'killer application'. The site had twelve thousand users at the end of 1999, when its application to auctions caught on. Four months later, while Billpoint was still beta-testing its system, PayPal's figure had soared to a million. Three years on, PayPal was bought by eBay for $1.5 billion dollars.

> "Do you, as an occasional buyer and seller, need to register for PayPal? The answer, in the long run, is likely to be yes."

As eBay had become the only online auction site worth using, so PayPal, with over sixty million members, became the online payment option you had to have if you didn't want to lose sales. Until PayPal established itself, I used to get two or three spam emails a day offering me (a mere occasional seller) the opportunity to take credit cards. That business quickly dried up, as did the need to receive and send cash dollars for US sales and purchases. In 2003, $12 billion passed through PayPal's coffers.

PayPal UK launched in October 2003, making it much cheaper to take money out of your PayPal account and into your bank account (25p for amounts under £50, free for amounts over). Do you, as an occasional buyer and seller, need to register for PayPal? The answer, in the long run, is likely to be 'yes'. But there are still questions about what level of membership to choose.

When you *don't* need PayPal

If you're a small UK seller who doesn't want the minimal hassle of selling abroad and is happy to deal with postal orders and personal cheques, you can get by without PayPal. The same goes for buyers, although they will find themselves excluded from PayPal-only sales.

Many buyers still can't be bothered to register with PayPal. In its early days, the system offered an incentive: a $5 bonus for the new user and the same for the seller who signed them up, but that's long gone. Nevertheless, it's generally worth having a PayPal account (which means you'll be able to use it as a seller, too). Here's how to do it:

Registering

Go to:

• www.paypal.com/uk/

and click on 'Sign Up Now'. You then have to choose between a premier, personal or business account. Choose 'personal' (you can always upgrade). You'll be taken to a page that looks like this:

Fig 40. Registering with PayPal

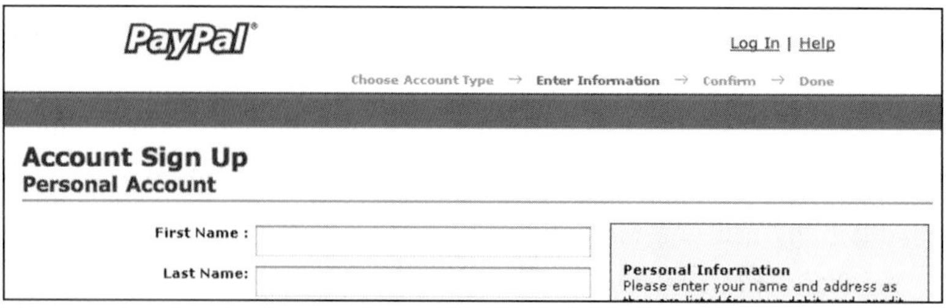

The signup process is easy. When you enter your information, you'll be asked to choose an eight character password and give the answers to two simple security questions in case you forget your password. Since this is an account where money is involved, it's a good idea to use a one-off password rather than one that you use for most of your net activities, tempting though that might be – it should have at least eight characters and no spaces. You'll need to give your telephone number and the country code for the UK, which is 44. You'll be asked whether you want a Premier account which allows you to take credit card payments. For now, decline. You can always upgrade your account later.

At the bottom of the page, you will be asked to read and agree to the user agreements and, finally, to copy out a unique number that appears on the screen as an additional security device. Then you should click on the 'Sign Up' button.

Once you've pressed the 'Sign Up' button, it will take a while for PayPal to check your details. If you have made any mistakes with the process, the form will reappear with a message in red at the top of the page, saying what the problem is. Any fields that you've filled in inadequately will also be highlighted in red.

Credit cards and email confirmation

You'll then be offered the opportunity to register a credit or debit card. You don't have to do this, and can do it later, but your account will have severe limitations if you don't attach a card to it (i.e. you will be able to receive money from other PayPal accounts, but only spend up to the balance of the *cash* in your account).

Once you have gone through this process (which includes taking a small amount from your card and asking you to confirm what appears on your next bill so that PayPal can confirm you are the rightful card holder) you will be taken to the final page, where you will be told that an email has been sent to your registered address. When you check your email, the message should already be there. Open the email, click on the link in it, and your PayPal account is active (you can receive payments, but won't be able to make them just yet).

Taking credit cards

Once you are registered with PayPal, you can take payments from buyers who have positive cash balances in their accounts – what they call 'funded accounts'. However, you cannot take payments from buyers who want to pay by credit card through PayPal. This is a tricky area, so follow closely.

PayPal makes its money in two ways. The first is by holding onto the cash which account holders have in their PayPal accounts and not paying interest on it. The second is by enabling account holders to pay for items by credit card and by charging the *sellers* fees on those card transactions.

If you, as a seller, want to be able to take credit card payments through the PayPal system, you have to be a verified 'Premier account holder'. **This costs 3.4% of the total transaction plus 20p** – not a huge cost, but not an insignificant one either. Evidently it works out slightly cheaper than taking credit cards directly. In other words, you're paying roughly the same as it costs a restaurant when a customer pays by credit card rather than cash.

Let's say that you *don't* want to take credit cards. That's fine. I got away with this for a long time. But it puts off buyers. And PayPal doesn't help you to avoid credit card payments. In the 'Accepted payment methods' box of your item description, you can put 'PayPal (from funded accounts only)' or similar, but sooner or later, somebody will try to pay you with a credit card. When that happens, you have a choice: you can reject the payment (leading to payment complications and possible buyer annoyance) or you can, as PayPal urges, upgrade to a Premier account so that you are able to take credit card payments. Be warned – there is one large drawback to taking this last course of action . . .

Premier accounts

When I first got paid with a credit card, I upgraded my PayPal account. But I'd made a stupid assumption. I thought that fees would only apply to those payments funded by credit cards. They don't. **If you have a Premier account you pay fees on every payment you receive** (this can include refunds, which seems particularly unfair). They don't publicise this, but PayPal does allow you to downgrade from a Premier account, but only once. There were a lot of complaints in the early days, but now most sellers bite the bullet, accept credit cards and stomach the fees that go with them. However, payment by credit cards has another implication, which is good for buyers, less so for sellers: chargebacks.

Chargebacks

The banks that issue credit cards offer their users automatic protection that far exceeds eBay's own anti-fraud systems. If an item doesn't arrive, or turns up faulty, buyers can ask the credit card provider to do a 'chargeback' on their account. Put simply, the bank takes back the money which PayPal has charged, and recredits it to the buyer's card account.

At the time of writing, PayPal has no choice but to go along with a chargeback. All it can do is try to recover the refunded amount from the *seller's* PayPal account. If, however, the seller does not have enough money in their PayPal account – if, indeed, they have gone AWOL, having emptied their PayPal account first – there is little that PayPal can do. It loses out. (In its early days, PayPal lost $8.9 million in chargeback charges to a Russian and Nigerian crime syndicate, so they are understandably twitchy on this issue.)

Note that, while Visa and Mastercard transactions can be disputed when PayPal customers suffer fraud, this doesn't apply to all credit cards. For instance, Discover and American Express transactions can't be disputed (a distinction that doesn't appear on PayPal's website). This is because of the differing merchant agreements signed by PayPal with the various credit card networks. Visa and Mastercard require PayPal to accept responsibility as the 'merchant of record' in its transactions. So PayPal is liable to foot the bill when a customer does not receive the merchandise and disputes the transaction. Discover regards Paypal as a 'middle man' with no responsibility beyond moving the money.

For obvious reasons, PayPal is unhappy when buyers use chargebacks to get their money back on an eBay transaction that goes wrong. It would far rather they used eBay's own grievance procedures. As a buyer paying with a credit card through PayPal, you are entitled to exercise a chargeback, but be aware that if you do, you will probably get an email from PayPal saying that if you do it again in the near future it will close down your PayPal account.

Protection

In 2004, eBay launched a new kind of PayPal protection in the UK. You can spot whether it applies to an auction you're bidding on by looking for the icon below.

Sellers are only allowed to put this logo on their accounts if they have more than fifty feedback points and have a positive rating of at least 98% (in other words, you can't screw up more than one time in fifty).

The service offers buyers coverage of up to £500 or $1,000 on an item. You must file a complaint within thirty days (this is common across eBay's complaint procedures). PayPal Buyer Protection is limited to three claim awards per user, per calendar year. (eBay's much more limited standard purchase Protection Programme allows three claims per user, per six months.)

Before filing the claim, eBay encourages buyers to work directly with sellers because most issues can be resolved through direct communication. Only when that fails should this policy apply.

Eligibility

For Buyer Protection to count, items must have been paid for with PayPal and paid to the seller's email address associated with the listing (reached through the grey 'Pay Now' button you see when the listing closes on eBay). The item must either have not been received at all or received in significantly different condition from what was described in the eBay listing. The items should be tangible items (physical goods that are delivered to you only). Services and intangible items (such as downloads) are not covered.

Limits

You may only file one claim per PayPal payment and claims must be filed within thirty days of the PayPal payment. The system does not cover cases where you are merely disappointed with the item you have received. If you claim fraud, you have to be willing to cooperate with PayPal's investigation by providing full information. If PayPal can't obtain the information it needs, the case may be cancelled without a refund.

You are limited to three PayPal Buyer Protection refunds per calendar year. If this limit is exceeded, PayPal can't guarantee full recovery of the purchase. **You will be awarded only what PayPal is able to recover from the seller.**

This last point is crucial. If the seller is a scam artist who has disappeared by the time you get round to making your complaint, Buyer Protection won't help. Your only alternative will be to do a credit card chargeback, with all the hassle and aggro that causes. This option remains even after the thirty day limit has expired. Understandably, eBay would rather you didn't use it, which is doubtless one reason behind the PayPal Buyer Protection policy.

The big freeze

PayPal, despite its cosy name, is shaping up to become one of the world's biggest financial institutions. It has been the victim of several large scale frauds and has had court cases against it over issues too complicated to waste time on here. The major complaint you hear against PayPal (apart from the credit card fee issue) is that it is prone to freeze the accounts of big account holders for reasons that the holders do not regard as fair. It's hard to know how seriously to take these stories. Most of them sound apochryphal.

It's undoubtedly the case that PayPal is forced to comply with money laundering legislation so has to do more stringent tests on larger accounts. If the account turns out to have faked information, it is within its rights to suspend the account until the user information can be verified. I don't hold with the conspiracy theorists who suggest that PayPal is not letting its customers get their hands on their money so that PayPal can earn lots of interest on it; PayPal has so much money to hold onto that it has little motive to do so fraudulently. But note that PayPal does make a lot of its money from interest payments and it may be worth paying the small fee to move money from your PayPal account to your bank account (especially as you have more protection when paying with a credit card than when you pay from your cash balance).

To PayPal or not to PayPal

There are no solid arguments against buyers using PayPal. You may be best off not keeping funds in your PayPal account but using it as a credit card account with the extra protection the card provider gives (warning: credit card terms and conditions change).

As a seller, you will also want to take PayPal, because it brings you more buyers and saves a lot of time. Also, people tend to spend more when they're able to use credit.

Until June 2004, sellers were allowed to add a surcharge, not exceeding the actual cost of PayPal's fees, for buyers who used PayPal funded by a credit card. It was never a particularly good idea to do so because surcharges put off buyers and do nothing to enhance your reputation as a seller. The practice is now outlawed. The policy is set out in Appendix 5 on pages 171-173.

Whether, as a seller, you upgrade to a Premier account or not is a close call. You need a Premier account in order to be able to take credit card payments, remember. If you're going to be more than an occasional seller of goods that often leave the UK, you're going to need a Premier account sooner or later, but you should probably put it off until somebody tries to pay you with a credit card and forces the issue.

Problems

If you have a problem with a PayPal payment, you can write to them via their contact page (listing topic, subtopic and specific question) at:

- www.paypal.com/uk/cgi-bin/webscr?cmd=_contact

or phone (with the usual time-consuming automated menu that you have to go through) on 08707 307 191 (national call rates apply and be prepared for a long wait).

To contact eBay, again you have to go through the contact pages at:

- pages.ebay.co.uk/help/contact_us/_base/index.html

which will force you to define the terms of your query even more closely before allowing you to write an email. In my experience, you do get a reply within twenty-four hours, as promised, but, if your query is PayPal related, you can be bounced between eBay and PayPal, which is a little annoying when the former owns the latter. Evidently, eBay cannot access PayPal accounts.

Using pictures and HTML

. . . .

Should you add a picture to your item?

Pictures aren't absolutely essential to all eBay listings. However, the first picture you use isn't charged for, so you may as well use one when you can. Some items do require a photograph: if you're selling a car, any kind of art work or something that can be described as a 'one-off', you're going to need a photo of the actual item in digital form on your computer for uploading to eBay. That means you'll have to buy or borrow a good digital camera (no point in getting a cheap one – a bad digital image is worse than no image at all). Depending on the kind of items you sell, a scanner may also be useful. You can scan print photographs or even do a freeze-frame capture from your video camera if you have the right connections and software, but the quality may not be up to scratch. Many high street camera stores also offer photograph-to-CD Rom transfer services.

Taking images from elsewhere

If you use eBay's Picture Services, explained overleaf, eBay will resize your pictures to a standard format. That's fine in most cases, but if you want something superior, and you want to save money, you can link to an image hosted on your own web space. Many internet service providers include some free web storage as part of their package. But note, it's an absolute no-no to piggyback on an image by putting in a link to somebody else's web space. It's an equally big no-no to steal pictures from someone else's site (or auction) and use them as your own. You can get NARU'd for this.

Stock images

Stock images are images of an *example* of an item, rather than the actual item being sold. Sellers use stock images all the time because it saves time and requires less expertise than using a digital camera. When selling something in a listing you illustrate with a stock image, your image should have 'stock image' written beneath it. This matters less if you're selling a CD, than it does if you're selling, say, an exercise bike.

The issue of where it's safe to take stock images from is a grey area. Images from the website of the company that made the product you're selling may, in many circumstances, be safe to use. Images from an original digital photo in another auction almost certainly aren't, even if your item is identical. Many sellers put watermarks on their images to stop them being appropriated. If you start using self-made images a lot, you might want to do this yourself. It's not worth making a meal of it, though – most watermarks are easy to remove with the right software.

The basics of using pictures

1. It should be clear in the photo what you're selling.

So don't clutter the photo with other objects or a distracting background.

2. Make sure that the image is in focus.

As well as making sure the picture is in focus, you should clearly show any aspects of the item that you particularly need or wish to highlight. Avoid flash reflections by using good lighting. There's a lot of software around (you probably got some free with your scanner or digital camera) that allows you to improve images. You'll decide for yourself whether it's worth exploring the intricacies of Adobe Photoshop and the like, but remember your original photograph has to be an accurate rendition of the item you're selling, or you could be in trouble.

---

3. Save your photo as a 'jpeg' file.

'jpeg' or 'jpg' is the internet-standard format for images. The 'Save As' drop-down menu should include this option and files should then be named with '.jpg' at the end. Note that merely renaming the file with '.jpg' at the end will not make it a jpeg, you must use 'Save As'. eBay Picture Services also accepts photos saved as BMP (.bmp file extension) and GIF (.gif file extension). If you use Internet Explorer, they will accept animated GIFs.

4. Keep your picture file size reasonably small.

Remember that not everybody has high-speed broadband so long image download times can be a serious drawback. eBay advises that picture file sizes should be no more than 50kb and, in display terms, no larger than 4" by 6" (i.e. standard photo size). If you use its basic service, eBay will automatically resize your photos to 400 x 300 pixels to speed upload and download time. For some items, it may be preferable or even necessary to put several images on your auction (current cost: 12p per extra photo). eBay offers a variety of ways to do this, including, for an extra charge, a kind of carousel slide show system and the ability to click to see close-up or larger images. These tend to be used only on the more high-end, potentially expensive sales.

Uploading pictures to your auction

The easiest way to host pictures on an eBay auction is by loading them from your computer onto eBay's Picture Services. You do this when first entering details of the item you want to sell. The third part of the 'Sell Your Item: Enter Pictures & Item Details' page looks like fig 41.

Fig 41. Loading a picture from the 'Sell your item' page

First picture is free. Click on 'Browse', then select the image file from your hard disc.

Additional pictures cost you money - currently 12p each.

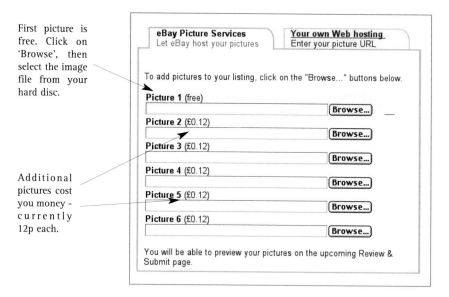

All you have to do is click on the 'Browse' button on the page shown above which will then give you a list of what's on your desktop. Select your picture (or pictures), make sure it's the right way up, and wait for this to pop up:

Fig 42. Uploading page

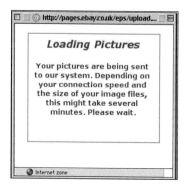

Screenshots on this page and opposite reproduced with the permission of eBay Inc.
COPYRIGHT EBAY INC. ALL RIGHTS RESERVED

Unless you're loading a full set of very large photos, this process will probably take less than a minute. When the page opposite appears, you're done.

Fig 43. Screen showing that your picture has been uploaded

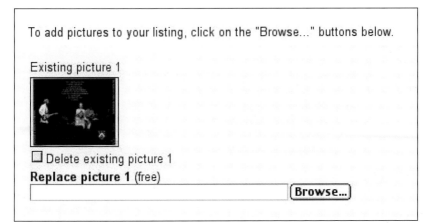

To add pictures to your listing, click on the "Browse..." buttons below.

Existing picture 1

☐ Delete existing picture 1
Replace picture 1 (free)

[   ] [Browse...]

Hosting pictures on your own web space

You don't have to use eBay picture hosting. If you prefer not to, all you have to do is click on 'Your own Web hosting' as shown in fig 41. and enter the website address of your hosted picture.

Other points to note

A couple of warnings:

- If you're listing more than one auction and click on 'Sell a similar item' then the image used for the first item will appear as the default image for the second item. Unless the items are identical, you will need to replace the first image with one that matches the second item.

- While it's easy to change an image before an auction goes live, it's impossible to change the image afterwards. Put the wrong photo up and your only way out is to cancel the auction.

Advanced picture features

Once you get started, you may want to move onto some of eBay's more advanced picture features. These allow you to crop, rotate and edit images, amongst other things. 'Supersize pictures' allows you to grab bidders' attention with larger photos that may be necessary for particular kinds of item. It allows you to display all your pictures up to 880 x 600 pixels. Images have to be at least 440 pixels wide by 330 high in order to qualify for the Supersize option. It currently costs 50p.

Using HTML

HTML can jazz up your listing and be used to link photographs (instead of using the 'Your own Web hosting' button mentioned earlier); it can also make your listing look garish and amateur.

The only HTML I ever use are the codes for **bold** and *italics*. To get these effects in your listings, simply type either <strong> or <em> before the word you want emphasised and </strong> or </em> afterwards. If you know what you're doing with HTML or have a decent programme that allows you to create interesting looking web pages, then good luck to you.

If you want to experiment with using the more basic HTML tools, then look at eBay's HTML tips that are linked off the 'Describe your item' page. When using HTML it's crucial to check how your description looks before loading it. Use the 'Preview your description' link. If you want to try out HTML without going through the eBay selling pages, there's currently a free practice board at:

- www.practiceboard.com/

Frauds, scams, deadbeat bidders and vigilantes

· ·

There's one born every minute

Once you have a PayPal account, people will try to steal from you. But it's not personal. Every day, millions of fraudulent emails are sent out purporting to be from eBay or PayPal. Some are in appalling English and include mistakes that should be a dead giveaway. Others look and sound like the real thing. Often they'll ask you to link to an 'official' eBay web page where you'll be asked to 'update your contact details'. There, you'll be asked for your password, credit card number and other sensitive information.

The first time I got one of these emails I went to the site, which was cleverly designed, with a half convincing URL, so that it looked like an official eBay site. (Some of the links on the fake page took you to the official site, making it even more convincing.) However, the form was asking me for information that I'd never give over the net, and I recognised it as a scam. The thing is, HTML is easy to copy and also makes it simple for fraudsters to disguise the origin of an email. The internet is the natural home of con men. Why target one potential sucker when you can email several million of them in a few seconds?

How to recognise scam emails

eBay does not send out emails addressed to 'Dear PayPal user' or 'Dear eBay member'. It uses your real name, the one you registered with. And it never asks you to give your password to bank accounts or, indeed, any password other than your eBay password and PayPal password when you want to access your personal pages. The only circumstance in which it is likely to ask you to 'update your contact information' (a frequent gambit used by scammers) is if there is a problem with one of your transactions and the other party is trying to contact you, but has found that your phone number doesn't work (you can have your account suspended for giving false contact information, but it is unlikely to happen unless you are deliberately falsifying your contact details, rather than forgetting to update it).

Below is an example of a fraudulent phishing email that I received while I was revising this book. I was having a problem with accessing a PayPal payment at the time and clicked on the link. The grammatical error ("You're" instead of "Your") should have alerted me, but I didn't notice it. What I did notice was that I was being taken to a page with a URL that was unrelated to eBay. I was then asked to sign in, with my PayPal password, and could have, effectively, given someone access to my credit card. Always be careful with online payments, in any situation. Most mistakes, in my experience, are caused by haste.

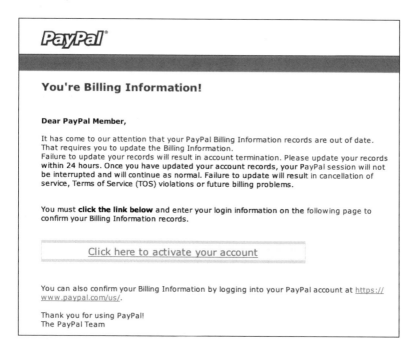

If you are in any doubt over whether an email is genuine, don't respond to it. Report it to spoof@ebay.co.uk and access your account in the normal way. If anything does need updating, update it, but only on the eBay site, never by email.

Fraudulent sellers

There are fraudulent sellers on eBay. The feedback system and eBay's security policies should ensure that they don't last long, but, where there are easy pickings, crooks will always find a way to return, and there will always be some newbies who fall for the most obvious of scams. This section offers some tips on how to avoid falling into those traps.

Study the seller's feedback and look out for any suspicious patterns. If the seller claims to be a store of some kind, check them out off eBay, by conducting a web search or even a Google Groups search. The first will indicate if they really are an active trading company and the second should tell you if there are many customers complaining about them.

> "If you are in any doubt over whether an email is genuine, don't respond to it. Report it to spoof@ebay.co.uk."

The long fraud

The most effective fraud you'll find on eBay is a variation of what is known as the 'long' fraud. The seller sets up an account, runs it honestly, building up positive feedback and then, after months or even years, starts to sell non-existent or fake goods (often of a kind which are much more expensive than they usually sell). By the time the negative feedback starts rolling in, the seller has gone. This is one reason for checking a seller's feedback even if the negative proportion is very low indeed. It could be that all of that negative feedback has arrived very recently, indicating the seller has just gone off the rails (or, as sometimes happens, had their account hijacked by a fraudster who has hacked their email account and password). Also, you can generally tell from the feedback (or by searching 'completed auctions') what kind of goods the seller usually sells. If they have moved from a low-cost to a high-cost item (particularly something currently fashionable like, say, iPods) be suspicious.

Vouchers, not the thing itself

Another frequent scam is that you'll see high-value items (such as iPods or laptops) being sold ridiculously cheaply. However, when you go to the description page, you see that the item being sold is not the thing itself, but a voucher or even an email address that supposedly allows you to get the thing cheaply (or, more likely, enter a draw to get one). You get what you pay for, or, in situations like this, a lot less.

Multiple User IDs

eBay does not bar users from having multiple User IDs – in other words, more than one identity on eBay. There may be legitimate reasons where it's appropriate to do so. But it does bar users from letting those User IDs interact with each other, for instance by using one identity to bid on the other identity's auctions, or using one identity to leave positive feedback about the other. Remember, the use of cookies means that eBay can often tell who you are no matter which ID you're using. You can disable cookies on most net browsers, but then you'll have to type in your User ID and password many, many times.

When a buyer breaks the rules

It's not just sellers who can break the rules. There are a number of bidding offences, such as auction interference, where somebody emails bidders in an open or finished auction to warn them off either the item or the seller. Bidders are not allowed to contact a seller asking them to sell the item off eBay, hence avoiding fees (and a fair auction). Bidders who try to discover another bidder's maximum bid by bidding absurdly high then retracting are also breaking the rules (hard to prove the first time, but an easy pattern to spot if anybody looks at the number of bid retractions on the offender's feedback page).

Unwelcome bidding is also against the rules – that is, bidding in a way which the terms of the auction do not allow (e.g. you're in the wrong country) or the seller has made it clear to you that they do not want you to bid, maybe because you have bad feedback or you have failed to complete a transaction with the same seller before. In each of these cases, the seller can report the buyer to the eBay Investigations team (a link can be found in several places, including under 'Safe Harbour', which is linked off the site map). The URL is:

- pages.ebay.co.uk/help/community/investigates.html

Shill bidding and other offences

'Shill bidding' means using a secondary ID (or an accomplice with a fake ID) to try to turn an auction to your advantage.

Seller shill bidding

The typical shill tactic by a seller would be to bid on their own auction with a second ID, egging on other bidders, and so increasing the final price for the item.

Buyer shill bidding

The typical shill tactic by a buyer would be to use their second ID to put in a bid which is so high that it puts off other bidders. Meanwhile, they use their real ID to manoeuvre into the position of second highest bidder. Late on in the auction, they retract the 'fake' bid, allowing them to win with their real ID bid. If it works, they scare off other bidders and get a bargain.

eBay has automated tools to identify shill bidding, but the majority of cases are reported by other eBay users. Anecdotal evidence suggests that it's still a serious problem, though I have to say that I've never experienced it from either side (but then, as a buyer, you wouldn't know if you'd been taken).

eBay's Investigations team will also look at the following situations:

- ✗ Theft
- ✗ Account theft
- ✗ Fee avoidance
- ✗ Chronic failure to complete auctions by shipping goods to the winner
- ✗ Misrepresenting yourself as an eBay employee or another eBay user
- ✗ Giving false contact information (including fake or discontinued phone numbers and email addresses)
- ✗ Underage users

Contacting the bidders in an auction and offering the same item more cheaply is against the rules, as is any attempt to interfere with eBay's software or auctions (by making fake bids to artificially inflate the price when you have no intention of paying).

Sending spam email to eBay members is against the rules. So is sending threats, using offensive language and publishing the contact details of another eBay user (tempting as this might be if they have defrauded you and you want to warn others).

You can be NARU'd for any of the above offences.

Sellers beware

If a buyer doesn't pay, you should follow the advice about 'Non-Paying Bidders' in the 'Advanced buying and selling' section. As a seller, the only ways you can lose money on eBay are if you part with goods before receiving payment and it never arrives, if you accept a cheque as payment and it bounces or if you accept payment by credit card and it is subject to a chargeback.

PayPal can take money from your account if a credit card company grants a buyer a chargeback and reclaims the money from PayPal. This can also happen if PayPal accepts a credit card that turns out not to be valid. Arguably, the seller should not be penalised in the last situation and the rules aren't concrete, but it's not a position you want to let yourself get into.

If you check your buyer's feedback you should be able to see if they normally buy the kind of thing you're selling. Extra care is required when sending expensive items. The enormous prevalence of credit card fraud means that many sellers are reluctant to sell to Africa or the Far East for fear of sending the goods and then finding their PayPal account subject to a chargeback. Chargebacks *should* only happen if you're at fault, though there are sellers who claim to have had funds removed from their PayPal accounts unfairly. Most experienced sellers keep their PayPal cash balance low to guard against chargebacks.

Cheque fraud

An increasingly common fraud involves buyers sending a large cheque for expensive goods – so large, in fact, that it is more than they are meant to be paying. The buyer makes a lame excuse for the overpayment and asks the seller to refund the difference (typically to a bank in a country other than their own) when the cheque has cleared.

'Fine', thinks the seller, waiting for the funds to be credited to their account before sending the refund. The funds appear, and the refund is sent. Then the buyer's cheque bounces. The problem is that UK banks often allow users to draw on cheques before they have fully cleared – typically within three working days. Yet it can take two weeks or more for a cheque to bounce. This fraud has become even more prevalent since the first edition of this book and most banks remain remarkably cagey about when a cheque is fully cleared. If in any doubt, don't send the goods.

Remember those Dan Dare books I sold in section 5? One of them was paid for with a cheque that, a fortnight later, was returned to me. I'd made a rookie mistake, not checking the date on the cheque. In the meantime, my account had been credited and then debited. Luckily, the buyer had made an honest mistake and quickly replaced his (accidentally) post-dated cheque with a valid one.

Often, the crooks who send rubber cheques aren't interested in the goods they buy, but in the money they can get from the seller. **Any request for money to cover an overpayment is almost certainly fraudulent.** Bank terms and conditions vary and a bank that cashes a fraudulent cheque does not have an automatic right to get the money back. If you have any doubts over a cheque payment you can request special clearance (usually for a small fee). Even better, if a significant amount of money is involved, insist on a building society cheque, banker's draft or electronic transfer (some of my correspondents favour the latter, although are wary because it involves giving out bank account numbers). Passwords and the bank's internal security measures should cover you here. Setting up a bank account just for your eBay payments may be over-cautious, unless you become a high volume seller.

Buyers beware

Buyers are more at risk than sellers. That said, in five years of trading on eBay, I've only been ripped off once (I'll use that as an example later in this section). eBay has protection policies in place but, in my experience, they give the buyer relatively short deadlines for making claims, while providing plenty of opportunities for the seller to stall. So, before we explore those policies, the best advice is not to buy from anybody who looks dodgy. Check feedback, ask questions if you see something suspicious and don't bid if there's no reply or the answer is unsatisfactory. If an auction looks so tempting that you want to bid on it despite severe doubts, bear in mind that, if it looks too good to be true, it probably is. Maybe you've found an inexperienced seller who's about to hand out a bargain, but be aware that you're taking a calculated risk.

eBay's buyer protection policies

SquareTrade

If a seller doesn't respond to your emails with a reasonable explanation of where your purchase is, you should try to use eBay's protection systems. You should also act quickly. The independent **SquareTrade** system allows you to exchange emails in a secure forum or pay twenty dollars (a fee subsidised by eBay) to employ a professional mediator. The use of SquareTrade may help you to resolve disagreements over, say, refunding a portion of the cost of an item that is in worse condition than described or which has been damaged in the post, but a serious fraudster will use it as a delaying tactic.

In most cases, you're best off going straight to eBay's Buyer Protection Programme. But there are two things to note. Firstly, eBay charges a fee (effectively, what insurers call 'an excess') of £15 in any claim, so it's not worth claiming for items that cost less than or only a little more than this. Secondly, if you paid for the item with a credit card, eBay will not reimburse you unless the credit card company has already turned you down (and, given that the credit card won't charge you £15, you should try to do a chargeback first). Since the maximum amount you can claim is £120 (less £15), you should make sure that you pay for items over that amount with a credit card.

Fig 44. SquareTrade

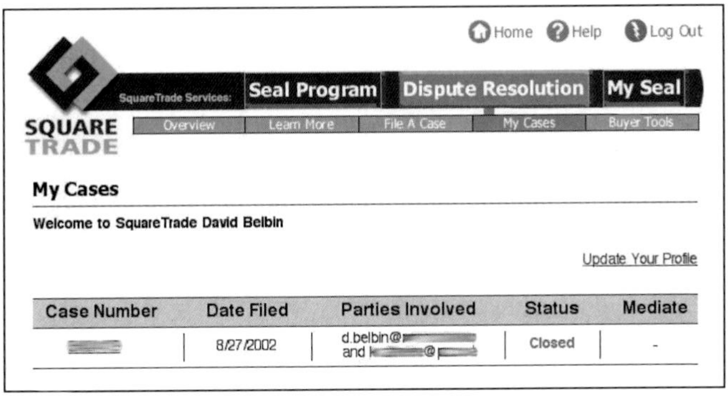

				Home Help Log Out

SquareTrade Services: **Seal Program** **Dispute Resolution** **My Seal**

SQUARE TRADE | Overview | Learn More | File A Case | My Cases | Buyer Tools |

My Cases

Welcome to SquareTrade David Belbin

Update Your Profile

Case Number	Date Filed	Parties Involved	Status	Mediate
	8/27/2002	d.belbin@ and k @	Closed	-

PayPal Buyer Protection

There is also the improved protection offered to buyers who use PayPal on auctions where this symbol is displayed. See page 126 for more details.

 PayPal Buyer Protection

Account Guard

Account Guard is a feature of the eBay Toolbar, downloadable at:

* pages.ebay.co.uk/ebay_toolbar/index.html

Account Guard warns users when they are on a potentially fraudulent (spoof) website. Unfortunately this feature is only available to PC users, and not to Mac users.

There have been attempted raids on PayPal's servers to harvest confidential data. However, eBay says that PayPal passwords, credit card numbers, and bank account numbers are protected because PayPal always encrypts this data and maintains it on secure servers that cannot be accessed by any merchant or third party.

More security measures

eBay advises that you regularly check your PayPal account for unauthorised activity and change passwords regularly. You should select a new password that uses a random combination of letters and numbers, avoiding using single names or words that can be found in a dictionary. PayPal passwords are encrypted and never shared with merchants or third parties. If you give your username and password to a sniping service, be very careful to establish that it is a genuine site and not a scam set up to harvest the details of your eBay account.

Furthermore, you should never download any email attachments that purport to be from eBay (indeed, you should never open any attachment that you weren't expecting to be sent). PayPal will never send an email attachment, or ask users to download anything from an email, in order to use its service or that of any partners.

Law enforcement

If a seller takes your money and doesn't send you the goods you bought, they're breaking the law. Regardless of how successful your eBay claim is, you should report them to the appropriate authority. In the US, the FBI has a website where you can report sellers. There have been some high profile prosecutions but anecdotal evidence suggests that you won't get much, if any, response.

If the seller is in the UK, you are much less likely to get ripped off and the police are a little more likely to take an interest. If you get nowhere with them, it's probably worth making a complaint to the Trading Standards Institute in the area where the seller lives. You can find this information by going to:

- www.tradingstandards.gov.uk/

What you should do depends on how much you've lost and how much effort you're willing to put into getting the guilty party punished. If the amount you've lost is too small to get eBay compensation it's likely to be too small for other bodies to get involved too. However, if it turns out that your seller has a regular pattern of this kind of behaviour, then eBay should, and the Trading Standards office might, take an interest. That said, it's worth recognising that the main thing you do by making official complaints is make yourself feel better.

The one time I got ripped off

In 2002, I saw an auction for an early fanclub single by my favourite band, REM. The starting bid was $24.95 and the seller shipped internationally. I put in a bid and, perhaps because the item was missing its picture sleeve, I was the only bidder, winning the item for maybe a quarter of what it would go for with the original sleeve. A day later, the seller sent me an invoice for this amount and $3.70 postage. I PayPalled it to him with a note saying to let me know if he needed more postage money to cover the cost of airmailing the single to the UK.

A week went by. I heard nothing. I pulled the seller's contact details off eBay and rang him up. I got an answering machine. There was no response to my phone message or the emails I sent. I filled in a SquareTrade complaint and the seller responded, saying that he hadn't sent the single because I'd failed to send enough postage. I gave a lengthy reply (I could include it here, but SquareTrade is meant to be confidential, so I won't) and, foolishly, perhaps, mentioned that I was about to go on holiday and hoped to find the single waiting for me when I got back. On my return, it still hadn't arrived. Thirty days had gone by. I found that PayPal (not owned by eBay at the time) would not look at a claim after thirty days (as the seller doubtless knew).

Most of the money for the payment had come from my PayPal balance, with only a little taken from my credit card, so there was no point in trying to do a chargeback. And the cost of the single in sterling was roughly £15, so there was no point in pursuing eBay's protection policies. I rang the guy again and got a machine. I filed a complaint to eBay. It was never responded to. I sent a couple of emails to the seller, one on the anniversary of the purchase. Oh, and I got an email from SquareTrade saying that the case was now closed and they assumed it had been resolved satisfactorily.

What mistakes did I make?

I failed to get a price for posting to the UK (I'd asked for this but he didn't reply, which should have given me a warning).

I failed to check his feedback. He had a huge positive score, but this was in the days before eBay printed a user's *percentage* of positives beneath their score.

If I'd searched his feedback today (for, yes, this seller is still allowed to trade on eBay), I'd have found that the seller has 1145 positive comments, left by 909 different users, but he also has **65 negatives**, leaving him with a percentage rating of 93.3, way below the level at which I consider it safe to bid. Below are just a few of his damning negative feedback comments.

The first comment was written two weeks ago. The last, eighteen months ago – by me. 'Thief' isn't very eBayian language, but the guy hasn't responded with a retaliatory negative (he only responded to one of his 65 negatives, and has only ever left three negatives himself.) But nor have eBay NARU'd him, even though this seller frequently (maybe when it's inconvenient or he hasn't got as much as he hoped for the item) doesn't deliver items. Presumably, this guy comes through with enough sales to maintain his feedback rating in the 90s and keep eBay off his back. It's against eBay policies for me to reveal his email address, full name or address, so I won't. I've written off the mistake to experience and – touch wood – haven't been ripped off since. Most eBay sellers are honest, but some aren't. Always check feedback before buying.

Fig 45. Negative feedback I failed to spot

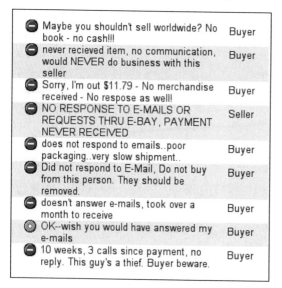

Maybe you shouldn't sell worldwide? No book - no cash!!!	Buyer
never recieved item, no communication, would NEVER do business with this seller	Buyer
Sorry, I'm out $11.79 - No merchandise received - No respose as well!	Buyer
NO RESPONSE TO E-MAILS OR REQUESTS THRU E-BAY, PAYMENT NEVER RECEIVED	Seller
does not respond to emails..poor packaging..very slow shipment..	Buyer
Did not respond to E-Mail, Do not buy from this person. They should be removed.	Buyer
doesn't answer e-mails, took over a month to receive	Buyer
OK--wish you would have answered my e-mails	Buyer
10 weeks, 3 calls since payment, no reply. This guy's a thief. Buyer beware.	Buyer

Vigilantes

If you see behaviour that breaks eBay's rules, you can report it by following the links on the bottom left hand side of the site map. If you're the copyright owner and want to get an auction removed (say because it's one of the bootleg CDs that flood eBay) you can join their VeRO programme (VeRO means verified rights owner). However, many auctions fall into more murky territory.

There are eBayers who, possessed of the original eBay spirit, take the law into their own hands. Vigilantes, if you will. They set up fake accounts and use them to bid up fraudulent or unethical sales, leaving the seller high and dry at the auction end.

The Glastonbury tickets saga

My internet buddy Hank is a senior social worker and, undisputedly, the UK's biggest fan of the US band, REM. In 2003, it was announced that REM would headline the Saturday night of the Glastonbury Festival. It was the first Glastonbury since eBay.co.uk got big. The auction site was one of the reasons why, for the first time ever, the festival sold out in a day (which it has continued to do). Many regular festival-goers were left without tickets. Some people decided to pay for their festival tickets by getting extras and selling them at a profit on eBay. A larger number, with no intention of going, bought Glastonbury tickets to sell on.

Hank's story

I was horrified when I looked on eBay to find that some of the bids on the tickets had already reached 3 or 4 times the face value. So I thought about what I could do. My previous experience in complaining to eBay directly about such auctions had not been positive. If they replied at all, it was to say there was nothing they could do so it was up to me!

I don't want to say anything too specific about the process of setting up a spurious eBay account. Let's just say that first I needed a verifiable email address that 1) couldn't be traced back to me and 2) wasn't provided by Hotmail or Yahoo! or one of the web-based providers. I then used this to create a 'new' eBay account which couldn't be traced back to me. With my newly created eBay identity, I was free to make ridiculously inflated bids for every Glastonbury ticket that was being auctioned on eBay.

"You want £200 for a ticket which only cost you £100? Here, take £500."

"You've got a high bid of £750 already for your 2 tickets? I'll bid £10,000."

"£150 for a car parking pass which cost you £40? I'll bid a quarter of a million. No problem."

With those high proxy bids in place, it was then possible for me and my friends to place legitimate bids using long established eBay accounts, secure in the knowledge that my alter ego had already placed a higher bid and that my legitimate bid would only serve to hike up the amount of the closing price. There was no way that any legitimate bid that I made would ever be successful.

After the auction ended, the sellers would be hit by either having to pay their percentage-based commission to eBay or having the nuisance of reporting my alter ego as a non-paying bidder. In any case, they would have had a short period of time when they may have genuinely believed that they were about to make a stupidly inflated profit on their tickets. Their resulting disappointment was, to me, justification for their actions.

My alter ego's account was – unsurprisingly – closed down by eBay after four weeks, but it was the work of ten minutes to set up another one. I probably bid on 40 auctions, always leaving the same feedback: "Touting Glasto tickets is a mortal sin." Come the day when any more Glastonbury tickets are touted on eBay, I'll be back there using this account and causing as much nuisance to the profiteers as I can!"

Ticket sales are a fast growing area on eBay and, given that many promoters don't offer refunds for returns, a useful service. But the phenomenon of people buying extra tickets for shows that are guaranteed to sell out so that they can auction them is ugly and sad. That said, it's merely another aspect of the 'perfect market' that eBay has created. Glastonbury has a 'peace and love' charitable ethos that isn't about the market and Michael Eavis has created safeguards (names and addresses on tickets, photo ID required) to ensure that touts can't easily sell tickets on. However, it's hard to see how ticket touting can be stopped.

Unless, that is, you're Bob Geldof. When tickets for the July 2005 Live8 gig appeared on eBay, Geldof went ballistic, ordering eBay to remove the auctions. Even before Geldof got involved, vigilantes bid millions to scotch the sales. This wasn't a charity event. Tickets were raffled in a text message lottery designed to cover the cost of the event. eBay, understandably, given their free market position, refused to remove legitimate auctions, but said that they would donate their profits to charity. Geldof said "it truly is filthy money they're making. We don't want it". He urged eBay employees to quit the company and eBay users to boycott it. Before the day was over, eBay changed their tune, and began removing the auctions.

Doug McCallum, eBay UK's managing director, said that there was conflict within the company's employees over how to handle this. They didn't take a moral stance on what they sold but they had listened to their members, who overwhelmingly wanted the sales removed. However, he told BBC Radio 4's PM programme on June 15th, "we're delighted to provide a vehicle for people who find themselves with a ticket they can't use to resell it". This ignores the phenomenon that eBay has created, where everybody can become a tout. Moreover, he emphasised that anyone making hoax bids would automatically have their account suspended.

The same day, I had to take a position on this in a TV interview. I praised the vigilantes, but said you can't expect eBay to take a moral stance, only a commercial one. It's for the government to take action. In 1994, selling on football tickets was banned because of the need to keep fans apart. If there's enough public will to stop ticket agencies charging rip-off service fees and ticket touts selling to the highest bidder, then government might act. I can't see it being very high on their list of priorities otherwise.

As a fan, what worries me even more than individuals selling tickets on is that, in the US, the biggest ticket agency, Ticketmaster, has been experimenting with auctioning the best tickets for top rock tours. I'm used to hitting the phone the minute tickets go on sale in order to secure the best seats. Generally, I can afford the most expensive seats for bands I like, but I can't outbid people who earn several times what I do. Maybe Ticketmaster will realise they're alienating their biggest customers. This has become one of the downsides of the 'perfect market' that eBay offers to buyers. eBay is not just about bargains. Where demand far exceeds supply, sellers will get the best price possible. And there's no going back.

Afterword

Since the first edition of this book, eBay.co.uk has passed the tipping point and become part of the *zeitgeist*. It's the most popular ecommerce site in the UK, and in the world. Any statistics I include here are likely to be outdated in the time it takes for a book to be printed. According to one documentary I watched recently, eBay now has a bigger turnover than the sixth largest country in Europe (or was it the world?). eBay appears endlessly in national tabloid and broadsheet newspapers. At first, the majority of these stories focused on fraud, even though reported cases of fraud on eBay are only 0.01% of all auctions. Later, as more journalists have become eBay users themselves, the stories have become fairer and better informed (though some still confuse the current bid price with the final selling price). Celebrities such as Cameron Diaz and Johnny Depp use the site, as does Cherie Blair.

eBay has also become an arena for a new kind of performance art. In the first edition, I wrote about a US auction for a used wedding dress, sold by a tattooed ex-husband who modelled it and used the auction to give a comic diatribe against his ex-wife. At one point, this auction was getting over a hundred hits a minute. The dress sold for $3,850, probably more than it cost. The final number of hits on the (regularly updated, as the seller got wedding proposals, appeared on talks shows etc.) auction page was over 16 million.

There was a UK equivalent to this auction, where a seller offered two invites to "a wedding I don't want to go to", garnering huge bids and a great deal of media, though many of the papers missed the final *denouement* of the auction, where the auction was withdrawn and the seller announced that he was going to go to the wedding after all, to try and persuade the bride-to-be to change her mind and marry him instead.

eBay has become a new way to tell stories, then – a pretty effective one, if publicity is the main thing you're after (me, I prefer royalties). But most of all, eBay *is* the story. The Stephen Joseph theatre in Scarborough even put on a musical about it.

In each newsworthy auction, endless bids had to be removed as fake bidders pushed the price into the millions. The charity auction of Jamie Oliver's

Aprilia scooter ended up open to 'preapproved bidders only'. The silly bid phenomenon is a result of the ease with which users can create new eBay accounts, as seen in the last section. The same thing happened to me, when I used my own account to auction (live, on air) a tie belonging to Radio 2 presenter Jeremy Vine, raising £930 for the BBC 'Children In Need' appeal. The whole thing was done at short notice, on a 1-day auction. There was no time to set up a preapproved bidders system. On air, hurrying between the studio and a computer in the next room, I prayed that a joke bidder wouldn't come in at the last second. Of course, someone did. (Why? Because they can.) Luckily, I was able to identify and contact the runner up, Nick Talley (see page 14) who was a genuine bidder (indeed, he later resold the tie in aid of 'Children In Need') and agreed, in the last minutes of the show, to honour his bid. (The full story of this auction can be found on my website, at www.davidbelbin.com – go to the archive for July 2004 and scroll down.)

eBay auctions can be a valuable publicity tool even if you have no intention of selling. One US store, Jay and Marie's, utilised a free 'Buy It Now' listing day to offer their (very successful) store for sale at a price of $5 million. It didn't sell, but created a lot of publicity for Jay and Marie's protest against the way that eBay was recategorising music sales, making it harder for the store's customers to find the items they were after. There are sites devoted to chronicling weird eBay auctions. Check out UK site www.rummaging.org for a good selection of current ones.

One of my favourite odd auctions involved a US seller who auctioned a twenty year-old Nintendo game console that he claimed was haunted by ghostly voices. It got 49 bids and went for $225 – at least ten times what such a console would normally be worth. In the UK, somebody tried to sell a "haunted" flat. Rather than list it in the (at the time of writing, underused) property section he put it in "everything else: metaphysical" and the auction was pulled. I've been on a radio programme with someone auctioning bottles of "genuine Huthwaite air" that people were bidding on (the bottles had a nice label, I suppose). On one of the proliferation of TV documentaries about eBay, the presenter sold some old rope he'd picked up on a beach. This list could go on and on and on.

According to a recent survey, Norwich has the highest percentage of eBay users in the UK. It's followed by Cambridge, Reading and Ilford. Nottingham, where I live, came sixth and Radio Nottingham rang me up to ask why. "I mean, we're the third most popular shopping city in the country," said the researcher. "You can understand places like Norwich – they're so boring, cut off, but why Nottingham?" I didn't have an answer, other than that Nottingham people like a bargain and I'd had a lot of local publicity for this book.

If you decide that eBay is far too much work for you, there are a growing number of sellers who will, for a commission, flog your stuff on eBay, often using their own eBay shop. You might think of this as a method of making money yourself, but bear in mind a couple of things: many people calculate that, to make any kind of real profit on eBay, you need to be making several pounds surplus per auction; also, selling things for friends is as easy a way to lose friends as lending them money, in fact, it's worse, because your reputation is the one at risk if there's anything wrong with the goods (or the friend changes their mind about selling after you get a bidder).

Should you, after reading *The eBay Book*, have any suggestions or corrections to make, I'd be grateful if you emailed them to:

editor@harriman-house.com

Please don't ask me questions: I don't have the time to research the answer and reply. As I've said elsewhere in this book, most questions about eBay can be answered by going to the discussion boards on eBay.co.uk itself or one of the newsgroups devoted to eBay.

eBay's a good way to clear out your attic, and fill the gaps in whatever you happen to collect. OK, it's easy to get carried away, wasting endless hours buying stuff you don't really need, but most users get over that phase quickly. On eBay, the thrill of the chase can be more fun than getting hold of whatever it is you thought you were after. But that still makes the site a cheap, harmless hobby at worst, and, at best, something much more useful. Ideally, eBay is a fair, friendly global market place that, like the internet itself, makes the world seem smaller and emphasises what people have in common rather than what divides them. Enjoy using it.

David Belbin

Appendices

• •

Appendix 1

Rules for buying and selling

Ten rules for buying

- Check feedback and don't bid if the seller has less than 98% positives.
- Always check the postage and packing costs.
- Bid your highest proxy as late as you can.
- Use the 'watching' facility on 'My eBay' to track auctions.
- Where possible, pay with PayPal backed by a credit card.
- Don't rush in with a high bid, there'll always be another one.
- If the price looks too good to be true, it probably is.
- If in doubt about an item description, ask the seller before bidding.
- Try not to get carried away and bid on items you don't really want.
- Remember, eBay is a community and work to make it work.

Ten rules for selling

- Don't use reserves.
- Make your descriptions as detailed as possible.
- Only use the best pictures.
- Answer bidders' queries quickly and candidly.
- Use advanced searches for essential pricing information.
- Keep clear, complete records.
- Choose end times to suit your item's buyers.
- Make your postage and packing terms clear and fair.
- Choose your auction titles carefully.
- Remember, eBay is a community and work to make it work.

Appendix 2

Selling cars on eBay

Since the first edition of this book, eBay has become the biggest source for second-hand cars in the UK, used by both dealers and private sellers. There are considerable advantages to selling on eBay as compared with going to a dealer or using classified ads. Your description can be much more detailed. You can deal with queries by email, rather than phone. There's no haggling involved and, since few bidders view before buying, you don't have to waste a weekend where people come to look over your car. You are much less likely to have to deal with time wasters. The set price listings are good value (and the fees are capped).

A car is sold at eBay Motors (motors.ebay.co.uk) every two minutes. If buying a car without going to see it first, you really must check the seller's feedback rating carefully (a lot of car sellers seem to be new users) as it's highly problematic pulling out if, when you turn up with the cash, the car is not as described (see Paul's story on page 11). There seem to be a substantial number of off eBay sales in car sales. Note that off eBay sales don't come with the usual safeguards, so be even more cautious than usual.

Appendix 3

Summary of eBay fees

1. Listing fees

When an item is listed for sale, eBay charges the seller listing fees. The amount depends on the type of listing, the minimum bid you set for the item, and whether or not you set a reserve price.

Auction listings

The listing fee will depend on the minimum bid you specify unless you specify a reserve price, in which case it will depend on that. The scale is shown below.

Minimum bid or reserve price	Listing fee
£0.01 - £0.99	£0.15
£1.00 - £4.99	£0.20
£5.00 - £14.99	£0.35
£15.00 - £29.99	£0.75
£30.00 - £99.99	£1.50
£100.00 +	£2.00

On reserve price sales there is an additional fee which is refunded to you if the item sells. This, too, is based on a scale:

Reserve price	Additional listing fee
£0.01 - £49.99	not available
£50.00 - £4,999.99	2% of reserve price
£5,000 +	£100.00
Motors	£3.00
Real estate	£2.00

'Buy It Now-only' listings

The listing fee is based on the 'Buy It Now' price, using the previous scale.

Notes

1. Special fee scales apply to motor cars (£6) and real estate (£35).
2. Stated fees include 17.5% VAT for UK residents.

Final value fees

Final value fees are the fees which you pay when your listing ends.

Auction listings

The final value is the closing bid. If there were no bids on your item, you do not pay any final value fees. The scale of fees is shown below.

Final value range	Fee percentage
£0.00 - £29.99	5.25% for the part of the current high bid up to £29.99
£30.00 - £599.99	3.25% for the part of the current high bid from £30.00 up to £599.99
£600 and up	1.75% for the balance of the current high bid greater than £600

Don't misinterpret this as meaning that the final value fee is 5.25% + 3.25% + 1.75% equating to 10.25% of the final bid. It isn't. In fact, the percentage decreases the more the item sells for. See the example opposite.

'Buy It Now-only' listings

The final value is the BIN price. If the item fails to sell, you do not pay any final value fees. The scale is the same as the one shown above.

Notes

1. Special final value fees apply to motor cars. At the time of writing they are:

£0.01 - £2,999.99	= £15	
£3,000 - £5,999.99	= 0.5% of final sale price	
£6000.00 and above	= £30 fixed	

2. There are no final value fees for items sold in the real estate category.

3. Stated fees include 17.5% VAT for UK residents. If you are a VAT-registered business, you may be able to get a VAT exemption.

4. Final value fees are calculated when the auction ends and are billed on a monthly basis, so sellers don't have to worry about tracking multiple small charges.

Example

In one of the case studies referred to earlier in this book, on page 10, Philip listed a Precor runnning machine for auction, setting a starting bid of £200 and a reserve price of £350. He also listed it in two subject categories. The running machine was sold at a high bid of £555.55.

The fee calculation on this transaction looked like this:

Starting bid: £200.00
Reserve price: £350.00
Final bid: £555.55

Listing fee Reserve price £350 is in the £100+ bracket so fee would normally be £2, but Philip listed the item in two categories so the fee was doubled to	£4.00
Additional listing fee for using a reserve The fee would normally be 2% of £350, but Philip listed the item in two categories so it was doubled to	£14.00
Final value fee (5.25% x £29.99) + (3.25% x £525.56) equals	£18.65

Total fees   £36.65

Points to note

1. Since the auction resulted in a sale, Philip was refunded his additional listing fee of £14.

2. If Philip had not set a reserve price, he would have saved himself £14 on the additional listing fee. The risk, though, would have been that the auction might have closed at a price well below the £350 he wanted.

3. Listing the running machine in two categories was expensive – the listing fee and the additional listing fee were both doubled.

Listing enhancements

On the 'Sell your item' page, sellers have the opportunity to raise the visibility of their listings and to enhance them in other ways. Each one costs money in extra fees.

At the time of writing the available options, and their costs, are as follows:

Homepage Featured	Your item is featured in a 'Special Featured' section and appears in rotation on eBay's homepage in turn with other featured items.	£49.95
Featured Plus!	Your item appears in the 'Featured Item' section of its main category and in bidders' search results.	£9.95
Highlight	Your item is highlighted in listings by a coloured background.	£2.50
Bold	Your item's title appears in bold.	£0.75
Gallery	A picture of your item appears in the Gallery, eBay's miniature picture showcase.	£0.15
Gallery Featured	A larger picture of your item appears at the top of the Gallery.	£15.95
Scheduled Listings	This enables you to list an item on eBay, but schedule the auction to start at a later date. You can do this up to 3 weeks in advance.	£0.06
Buy It Now	Use BIN in combination with an auction to allow a buyer to 'win' immediately if they offer the BIN price.	£0.06
List in 2 categories	Instead of having just one main category for your item, you can have a second category.	2 x normal listing fees

Paying fees to eBay

eBay lets you pay your fees in a number of ways:

1. Direct Debit

When you register with eBay you can elect to pay your fees by Direct Debit if you have a bank account in the UK. You have to fill out an authorisation mandate and post it to eBay, which then debits fees from your bank directly. As long as it is able to collect these fees, you can list as many items as you want.

2. Debit or credit card

An alternative to Direct Debit is to provide details of a credit or debit card, and to authorise eBay to bill the card monthly for the previous month's fees.

3. Pay-as-you-go

This method allows you to pay your monthly listing fees by cheque or postal order, or to authorise a one-off credit card payment. The disadvantage is that if the accumulated unpaid fees amount to more than £15, eBay will not let you list additional items.

4. PayPal

You can pay money into PayPal to cover any listing fees on your eBay seller account.

Every month you will get an email invoice from eBay which summarises your account activity in the previous 4 weeks and which shows you how much you owe eBay. If you have authorised Direct Debit or credit card billing, the amount will be collected by those methods automatically. If you are on Pay-as-you-go, it is up to you to arrange payment.

You can access your billing records by going through the 'Accounts' link on the 'My eBay' page.

Figures are correct at the time of going to press, but are subject to change.

Appendix 4

Bidding increments

A bidding increment is the amount by which the high bid on an item automatically rises under the proxy bidding system. The size of the increment depends on the current high bid on the item. The higher the current high bid, the larger the increment, as shown by the table below.

Current high bid	Bid increment
£0.01 - £1.00	£0.05
£1.01 - £5.00	£0.20
£5.01 - £15.00	£0.50
£15.01 - £60.00	£1.00
£60.01 - £150.00	£2.00
£150.01 - £300.00	£5.00
£300.01 - £600.00	£10.00
£600.01 - £1,500.00	£20.00
£1500.01 - £3,000.00	£50.00
£3,000.01 +	£100.00

Figures are correct at the time of going to press, but are subject to change.

Appendix 5

eBay's surcharge policy

On June 5th, 2004, the policy in the box below was put into place "in the interests of ensuring that all buyers receive clear and accurate pricing information when trading on eBay.co.uk". The policy applies only to items listed on eBay.co.uk. eBay regularly reviews its policies and, in due course, the policy below may be replaced by a different policy. Users should therefore check the website regularly to see what the current policy is.

Surcharge policy

eBay will prohibit surcharging by sellers except where described below. Surcharging occurs when sellers pass the charges they incur for using eBay or third party services such as payment services onto buyers. Specific examples are explained below for your guidance:

1. Electronic Money Services

Sellers who accept electronic money services as a means of payment for an item purchased on eBay may not impose a surcharge. Electronic money services include, but are not limited to, services such as PayPal, Nochex, FastPay or Moneybookers.

2. Cheques and Money Order

Sellers may not charge buyers an additional fee for their use of ordinary forms of payment, including acceptance of cheques and money orders.

3. eBay Fees

Sellers may not pass on to buyers any eBay selling fees including, but not limited to, listing fees, listing enhancement fees and final value fees.

Exceptions to the surcharge policy:

1. Credit and Debit Card payments

Surcharging is permitted where sellers accept credit or debit cards as a means of payment for an item purchased on eBay. Such sellers will have merchant accounts with a bank or credit card company.

These sellers may not pass on to the buyer a charge greater than the amount of the commission payable by the seller to the bank processing that credit or debit card payment. In other words, sellers may recoup the charges incurred as a direct consequence of accepting the credit or debit card, but no more.

Please note that under English law, sellers have a legal right to pass onto the buyer the charges incurred for a credit or debit card transaction. However, this right does not apply to electronic money services. Where a credit or debit card is used to purchase electronic money to fund a transaction made via an electronic money service such as the ones listed above, this is not a credit or debit card transaction, but an electronic money service transaction.

2. Posting and Handling

Sellers may add a reasonable posting and handling fee to the final price of their item, providing that this fee is disclosed up front in the listing. A posting and handling fee can cover only the seller's reasonable costs for mailing, packaging and handling the item. Posting and handling fees cannot be listed as a percentage of the final sale price.

3. Escrow

Sellers may pass along the costs associated with using a third party escrow service, if the buyer chooses to use an escrow service and if the costs are disclosed and agreed to, in advance, by the buyer.

4. Different Currencies

Sellers may choose to accept payment in a different currency from the currency listed on eBay. If the buyer chooses to take advantage of this optional payment method, the seller may pass along to the buyer any costs associated with the currency exchange, provided that the costs are disclosed and agreed to, in advance, by the buyer.

I've reprinted the policy in full, but the main change that sellers should note is that it is **no longer acceptable to charge a surcharge for taking PayPal**. As noted earlier in this book, many buyers are put off by surcharges, making it unwise to use them. According to eBay's own research, "68% of UK buyers say that they are less likely to buy from a seller who surcharges for accepting online payment via a service such as PayPal. These buyers will actively seek out similar listings that do not charge extra fees". From now on, as far as PayPal is concerned, sellers no longer have the option of surcharging the remaining 32%.

Appendix 6

Tax treatment of eBay income

General points

From a tax point of view, trading on eBay is no different to any other type of personal trading. The general points to note are:

1. There are no hard and fast rules about what kind, and what level, of trading is taxable and what is not.

2. In general, if your sales are confined to goods which you originally owned for personal use, and if their value is low, and if you are doing it as a hobby rather than as a business, the income and profits will not be taxable.

Crossing from non-taxable to taxable trading*

The factors that change eBay trades from being non-taxable to being taxable are:

a) Value

The higher the value of your trades, and the higher the profits you make on them, the more likely they are to be taxable. Profits of a few hundred pounds per year are probably not taxable. Profits of several thousand may well be.

b) Frequency

The more often you trade on eBay, the more likely the Revenue is to regard it as a business. The fact that you are in regular employment elsewhere does not mean that your profitable sideline on eBay is not also a business.

c) Nature of goods

If you only sell goods which you originally bought for personal use or inherited, the profits are unlikely to be taxable, even if you make large capital gains. If you are buying goods specifically to sell them at a profit, that's a business!

Ask HM Revenue & Customs

If you are in any doubt about whether your eBay profits are taxable, ask your local tax office.

*Note: the information on these pages is for guidance only. Readers are advised to consult an accountant or other suitably qualified professional if they think that their transactions on eBay may have tax implications.

Appendix 7

Record-keeping

Most of the information you need on your recent purchases and sales is stored on your 'My eBay' page. It shows items you've bought, items you've sold, items you're watching, and items you've bid on. Going to 'Accounts' will help you to check your eBay fees.

Another useful way of accessing old auctions where you've lost the details is by going through your feedback page. The item number appears alongside the feedback and the original auction page will stay online for approximately 90 days. (I don't know why eBay uses 90 day – or a month in some cases – time limits: perhaps, if they allowed users to look back further, the burden on eBay's servers would be too great. Or perhaps they're planning on charging for a premium service in the future.)

Not everybody leaves feedback and you may need records for more than 90 days, so it's a good idea to keep detailed records – either on your computer or on paper. If you don't back up your computer records on CD, disk or a server somewhere, you should probably keep paper records for at least a year. While your trading on eBay won't initially be frequent enough, or at a high enough value, to constitute a business which is declarable for tax purposes, one day it might. Should you need them, it's useful to have all the records in the right place. That way, you can provide accurate, verifiable information to HM Revenue & Customs. They probably won't appreciate being told to 'look on eBay', although they'll be able to check much of the information you give online. A bigger risk that requires you to keep good records is that of complaints, fraud and chargebacks.

The records you keep should include a note of when you dispatched goods to buyers, and how much sending the parcel actually cost in postage, and there is nowhere on eBay to do that. You may find that a form in which you record your transactions on paper gives a good 'at-a-glance' perspective of how you're doing that you cannot get from web pages. An Excel spreadsheet can be a useful tool as you can use its formulas to work out averages, overall profits and so on.

Useful web resources

eBay pages

Advanced search

- search.ebay.co.uk/ws/search/AdvSearch?sofindtype=1

Community boards

- hub.ebay.co.uk/community/

Glossary

- pages.ebay.co.uk/help/basics/g-index.html?ssPageName=EEX:Glossary

Site map

- pages.ebay.co.uk/sitemap.html

UK announcement board

- www2.ebay.com/aw/marketing-uk.shtml

UK charity auctions

- pages.ebay.co.uk/charity/

UK suggestion box (with link to customer support)

- pages.ebay.co.uk/community/suggestion/

User agreement

- pages.ebay.co.uk/help/policies/user-agreement.html

Other websites

Anti-PayPal site

- www.paypalsucks.com

Checking negative and neutral feedback of other users

- www.toolhaus.org/cgi-bin/negs

DeadbeatBuster – anti-fraud site

- www.deadbeatbuster.com

Don Lancaster's The Guru's Lair (lots of useful pdf downloads)

- www.tinaja.com

eBay hacks

- www.ebayhacks.com

Frequently asked questions site for the newsgroup uk.people.consumers.ebay

- upce.org.uk

Google UK

- www.google.co.uk

HTML practice board

- www.practiceboard.com

PayPal

- www.paypal.com/uk/

Royal Mail

- www.royalmail.com

USPS (for checking real cost of posting from US)

- www.usps.com

The references above are provided for guidance only. Neither the author nor the publisher can vouch for the accuracy of the information provided on them, or the quality of their services.

Appendix 9

Further reading

Books about eBay

eBay Hacks: 100 Industrial Strength Tips and Tools
David A. Karp, O'Reilly, paperback, 2005, £17.50

eBay: Top 100 Simplified Tips and Tricks
Julia Wilkinson, John Wiley & Sons, paperback, 2004, £13.95

The Perfect Store: Inside eBay
Adam Cohen, Piatkus Books, paperback, 2003, £7.99

Coming soon:

The eBay Business Handbook: The Complete Guide To Building A Business
and Making Money On eBay
Harriman House, paperback, 2005, £12.99

Related subjects

DK Collectables Price Guide 2005
Judith Miller, Dorling Kindersley, hardback, 2004, £17.99

Miller's Collecting Vinyl
John Stanley, Miller's Publications, paperback, 2002, £12.99

Miller's Sci-Fi and Fantasy Collectibles
Phil Ellis, Miller's Publications, hardback, 2003, £14.99

Superhobby Investing
Peter Temple, Harriman House, paperback, 2004, £14.99

These books can be ordered at a discount from the Global-Investor bookshop
by ringing 01730 233870 or by visiting www.global-investor.com.

Appendix 10

Glossary

Advanced search

A more detailed system than the standard eBay search box that allows users to make more specific and sophisticated searches.

Bid cancellation

See 'Blocked bidder' below.

Bid increment

The minimum amount by which a bid must be raised, determined by the current bid price.

Bid retraction

Where a buyer withdraws their bid on an item. This has to be done within a timeframe, giving legitimate reasons for withdrawal.

Bid shielding

When a 'buyer' (in league with a second buyer) posts an unusually high bid, only to retract it late on so that the second buyer wins the item for less than it might otherwise have gone for. Against eBay rules.

Blocked bidder

A bidder who is not allowed to bid on an auction because the seller, for whatever reason, has put them on their blocked bidders list. Any bid a blocked bidder attempts to make is automatically rejected. Sellers can, at any time, cancel a bid for any reason they choose.

Bulk listing

Listing large numbers of items for sale at once, using eBay's 'Turbo Lister' system or software obtainable from a third party.

Buy It Now

Either a set sale listing or the price at which, if the buyer pays it, the seller will stop the auction and sell the item (provided any reserve has been met).

Category

The classification system used by eBay where similar or related items can be found. Most categories are broken down into multiple subcategories.

Chargeback

Refund to buyer of the payment made by them from a PayPal account funded by a credit card, when the goods paid for have not been delivered.

Cookies

A token of agreement between cooperating computer programmes that allows the retention of information, usually including a username and the current date and time, that is stored on the web user's computer. Cookies are mainly used by websites to identify users who have previously registered or visited the site.

Deadbeat Bidder

Someone who successfully bids on an auction but does not follow through with their payment. Do this more than twice and the bidder is liable to be 'NARU'd' – see eBay acronyms below.

Discussion boards

Community question and answer boards where eBay users help each other out with pertinent information and gossip.

Dutch auction

Also known as a Multiple Item auction. The bidder specifies the number of items they're interested in and the price they're willing to pay. All winning bidders will pay the same price: the lowest successful bid.

Escrow

An escrow service will hold your payment until you've received, inspected and approved the item. Only then does the escrow service pay the seller. eBay recommends using Escrow.com (www.escrow.com) for purchases of £250 or more. Fees apply. Fake escrow services are commonly used by fraudsters.

Feedback

The comments left by seller and buyer after a transaction, together with a positive, negative or neutral endorsement. Commonly expressed as a percentage of positive comments, known as 'Feedback rating'.

Feedback exhortation

When a buyer or seller demands that an eBay user do something they are not required to do, threatening that otherwise they will leave negative feedback.

Feedback rating

The percentage of positive comments a buyer or seller has received in feedback. This rating is followed by a figure in brackets showing how many transactions the feedback is based on.

Final value fee

The fee a seller pays to eBay at the end of a successful auction, based on a percentage of the final sale price.

Gallery

An extra auction feature (at an additional cost) that gives a thumbnail image of the item being auctioned on the listings page, attracting buyers to view the auction itself.

Google

The world's most popular internet search engine, found at www.google.co.uk.

High bidder

The bidder who is currently winning the auction.

Keyword spamming

Where a seller places popular words in listing titles or descriptions and the words are irrelevant or misleading, in order to attract bidders to view their auctions. Against the rules.

Listing fee

The cost of an auction listing, also known as an 'insertion fee'. It is calculated by taking a percentage of the opening bid price and adding the cost of any other features (e.g. reserve, 'Buy It Now', gallery).

Maximum bid

The highest price a buyer is willing to pay for an item, submitted to eBay as a secret proxy bid.

My eBay

A web page where users can keep track of their eBay activities, watch items and access further information about eBay.

Neg

Short for 'negative feedback'. Also used as a verb, meaning 'leave negative feedback for'.

Newbie

New user of eBay or any activity to do with computers and the internet.

Newsgroups

Public discussion groups that can be accessed by dedicated newsgroup servers, email programmes and search engines (e.g. Google Groups). An example of a newsgroup is alt.online.marketing.ebay.

NPB

Non-paying bidder. See also 'Deadbeat bidder'.

Outbid notification

Email (or text message) sent by eBay to inform a bidder that another bidder has exceeded their maximum proxy bid and they have been outbid.

Phisher emails

Emails that pretend to be from eBay or PayPal and guide the recipient to a fake site that will try to extract user names, passwords and PIN numbers – information that should never be given out in an email or in any environment that is not 100% secure.

Power Seller

Sellers with a significantly high turnover and more than 98% positive feedback. There are five levels of Power Seller, from Bronze to Titanium. Power Sellers get their own icon and better support from eBay, including, at the higher levels, telephone access to an eBay staff member.

Preapproved bidder

Sellers can limit who is allowed to bid on each of their listings by creating a list of preapproved bidders who may bid on that item. Any bidder/buyer who is not already on the seller's list will be asked to contact the seller by email before being allowed to place a bid. Should be used warily but useful in auctions that are likely to attract spoof or fraudulent bids.

Private auctions

An auction where bidders' User IDs won't show up on the item or bidding history screens. When the auction ends, only the seller and winning bidder will know who bought the item. Not available for Dutch Auctions.

Private feedback

Where an eBay user refuses access to feedback comments left about them. Highly suspicious for the reasons given on page 68 of this book.

Proxy bid

The secret maximum bid that buyers submit to eBay, which will raise the bid to maintain the buyer's position as high bidder until the auction is over or the buyer's maximum bid is exceeded by another bidder.

Registered user

A member of eBay.

Reserve/Reserve auction

Where the seller sets a minimum price higher than the starting bid, below which they do not have to sell their item. Offputting to many bidders.

Secure server

A server using SSL encryption to process credit card and other online payments.

Scheduled listing

An auction listing that starts at a set time other than the time when the listing is submitted. A fee is charged for this service.

Shill bidding

When a seller places a bid on their own item, either directly or through others. Against the rules. Family members and people living together, working together or just sharing a computer are not allowed to bid on each other's items.

Sniping

Bidding in the last few seconds of an auction to prevent earlier bidders having time to raise their proxy and outbid the sniper. Increasingly prevalent with experienced eBay users and often achieved with automated programmes. Some sniping 'services' are fraudulent attempts to 'phish' for a user's eBay password and account details.

Star system

Coloured stars that appear next to a user name showing how much positive feedback the user has, from 10+ to 100,000+.

Starting bid

The lowest opening bid set by the seller in an auction.

Support boards

The official eBay bulletin boards on which users can post questions and get answers from eBay.

Usenet

An American word for the messaging system that uses the internet to transfer messages organized in thematic groups. See 'Newsgroups'.

User ID/User name

The name chosen by registered users that they are known by on eBay.

VeRO

An acronym for 'Verified Rights Owner'. Copyright holders who join the VeRO programme can complain about the auctioning of material to which they hold the copyright and have a listing removed.

Watching page

A page that allows you to follow the bidding on up to thirty auctions and link directly to them. Part of 'My eBay' – see definition above.

eBay's own glossary resources

eBay.co.uk has an A-Z index that can be found at:

- pages.ebay.co.uk/help/index/A.html

There's also a search box at

- pages.ebay.co.uk/help/index.html

where you can find explanatory pages on all sorts of eBay topics.

eBay.co.uk has its own glossary which can be found at:

- pages.ebay.co.uk/help/basics/g-index.html?ssPageName=EEX:Glossary

Chapter 1

Appendix 11

eBay acronyms

B&W: Black and white

BC: Back cover

BIN: Buy It Now

FAQ: A list of frequently asked questions with answers

FB: Feedback

FVF: Final value fee

GU: Gently used. Should be followed by explanation of wear

HP: homepage

HTML: HyperText Markup Language - the language used to create web pages

IE: Internet Explorer

INIT: Initials

ISP: Internet Service Provider - a company that gives you access to the internet

JPG: Preferred file format for pictures on eBay (pronounced 'Jay-Peg')

LTD: Limited edition

MIB: Mint in box

MIJ: Made in Japan

MIMB: Mint in mint box

MIMP: Mint in mint package

MIP: Mint in package

MNB: Mint no box

MOC: Mint on card

MOMC: Mint on mint card

MONMC: Mint on near mint card

MWBT: Mint with both tags

MWMT: Mint with mint tags

NARU: Not a registered user (i.e. a suspended user)

NBW: Never been worn

NC: No cover

NIB: New in box

NM: Near mint

NPB: Non-paying buyer

NR: No reserve

NRFB: Never removed from box

NWT: New with tags

OEM: Original equipment manufacturer

OOP: Out of print

PM: Priority Mail

RM: Royal Mail

S/O: Sold out

SIG: Signature

TM: Trademark

URL: Uniform Resource Locator - the address that identifies a website
           (such as www.ebay.co.uk)

USPS: United States Postal Service

VHTF: Very hard to find

Index

C

D

E

F

G

H

I

P

R

S

T

U